Mind Your Manners

A Guide to Good Behaviour

Mind
Your
Manners

A Guide to Good Behaviour

Robert O'Byrne

PRION

This edition published 2005 by
ANDRÉ DEUTSCH
an imprint of the
CARLTON PUBLISHING GROUP
20 Mortimer Street
London W1T 3JW

First published 2004 by
SITRIC BOOKS
62–63 Sitric Road, Arbour Hill,
Dublin 7, Ireland
www.sitric.com

A catalogue record for this book is available from the British Library.

ISBN 1 85375 578 8

Set in 10.5 on 13 pt Minion by Susan Waine
Printed by Creative Print and Design Group, Middlesex, Great Britain

To Kathy with thanks, naturally

Contents

Introduction

B asic good manners are so obvious that they shouldn't need any elucidation. They shouldn't, but all too often they do. Why is this the case? Why do we need to be told over and over again how to behave properly? Isn't it obvious?

The only purpose of good manners is to demonstrate courtesy and consideration towards people and to put everyone at ease. Good manners mean you behave towards others in the same way you'd wish them to behave towards you. It's a fundamental tenet of good manners never to be openly judgmental of another person's speech or behaviour.

It's easy to bemoan the lack of good manners today. What has actually been lost is the concept of consideration; manners are just the overt expression of this idea and a considerate individual will always have good manners. But it's important not to become too stuffy on the subject. The spirit of our age inclines towards the casual; we should do the same. Accept that we live in informal times when many of the rules that used to govern social interaction – rules generally based on traditional etiquette – have been discarded.

This ought to mean that we're all equally well behaved. Unfortunately, that's rarely the case. Don't allow this to affect you or your behaviour. Instead, recognize that politeness, courtesy and consideration are always going to be preferable to their opposites, no matter what the character of the age. Practise them and you'll be known – and appreciated – for your good manners.

Modern Manners: The Twelve Basic Rules

1. Whenever asking for anything, whether a dress in another size or a dinner date, always include the word 'please'. It's only six letters and one syllable but will make all the difference to the way in which you and your request are judged.

2. Two other words that ought to be a regular feature of your speech are 'thank you'. Every time someone does you a service, don't presume that your gratitude will be understood – make it audible.

3. After you've enjoyed someone else's hospitality, be it a cup of tea or a week's holiday, get in touch promptly and express your appreciation. Thank-you letters, whether they take the form of a phone call, text, email or card, should be received sooner rather than later, preferably within twenty-four hours.

4. Try never to arrive in anyone else's home empty-handed. Your gift doesn't need to be lavish, although even the simplest item should reflect the personality and tastes of the recipient.

5. Be a good customer – in shops, restaurants, etc. As a rule, employees in the service industry are poorly paid for working long hours in bad conditions, so no wonder they can sometimes appear indifferent. But rudeness on your part will not improve circumstances, either for them or for you.

6. Apologize immediately if you've done something wrong. Or even if you think that you've done something wrong. 'Sorry' is a small word, but it can make a big impression. So too can its absence.

7. Never make a promise or commitment you can't keep. Better to disappoint someone now than to raise hopes that'll be dashed later. This is especially applicable to all repairmen, plumbers and removal companies.

8. Be punctual. Only selfish people are habitually late.

9. In conversation, learn to listen. The best talkers are those who hear what's being said to them.

10. Encourage other people to talk about themselves. That way, you'll quickly gain a reputation for being charming.

11. Be cheerful. It'll make you feel better – and everyone else you meet too.

12. Remember the maxim: 'Do unto others as you would have done unto yourself.' And then apply it to your daily life.

I. Being a Good Guest

Y ou're seated next to a really delightful husband and wife at lunch and just before leaving the table they announce, 'We must meet again; feel free to drop in on us next time you're in the neighbourhood.'

Invitations

OPEN INVITATIONS
No matter how sincere their tone, don't take the offer seriously. Otherwise you'll turn up on their doorstep and be met with bafflement. On the spur of a particularly social – and often alcohol-enhanced – moment, we all invite people to our homes. These open invitations are lightly issued and, while much appreciated, they're better dismissed just as lightly. The only true invitation is one that comes attached to a specific date, time and place. Anything else is a pleasantry, implying a com-pliment to the charm of your company.

Sometimes open invitations are issued as though trapped on a loop-tape. Every time the two of you meet, the same person repeats the same line: 'You have to come round for brunch/lunch/ dinner/tea/recreational sex.' Unless the offer's much more pre-cise ('Fancy an hour between the sheets next Tuesday afternoon in an apartment that I've rented for the purpose?'), consider it flattering but worthless. If the person in question really wants to entertain you, he/she will make an effort to do so with a solid invitation.

How to behave if you took a casual offer to heart and have now arrived at someone's home? Expect to be unexpected. Few of us today entertain without plenty of advance notice and the well-groomed man you met at that party could now be wearing a grimy vest and slippers. Whatever food and drink is given to you will probably be meagre and prefaced with the apology, 'Sorry, but had we known you were going to drop by …'.

OOPS, YOU'VE FORGOTTEN AN INVITATION
While we're all afflicted by moments of memory-loss, some of us have discovered a convenient way of making sure this doesn't affect our social lives: it's called a diary.

You still forgot to go to a party? Telephone your erstwhile hosts as soon as you remember the invitation and be profuse with your apologies. Only do so if this was a genuine case of forgetfulness. It's a dangerous practice to use poor memory as an excuse when, in fact, you opted for a better offer, or just decided to stay at home and watch television that night.

BETTER OFFERS
Gregarious guests are faced with this dilemma sooner or later. In the typical scenario, you've just accepted an invitation – nothing particularly exciting, just a kitchen supper with a couple of old pals from college but it'll do because there was nothing else planned for Friday night. Then your mobile phone rings with the offer of something really special. For years, you've been waiting for the opportunity to be asked to a major film première, a small dinner with Jude Law or even the chance to meet someone you've been secretly lusting after (probably also Jude Law). Now that opportunity comes along and you have to turn it down.

That really is the only thing you're allowed to do.

Understandably, you'll be tempted to abandon your original commitment for the sake of the better offer. Particularly if one host is unknown to the other, you'll feel confident that the reason for your change of plan can remain forever a secret. No one will ever need to know the truth, you think to yourself, while mulling over various possible explanations you could offer for a sudden inability to attend the old college pals' kitchen supper.

But the well-mannered guest is a loyal guest. Resist the temptation to lie because dishonesty invariably proves a bad policy. Imagine how you'd feel were roles reversed and you were placed in the position of a disappointed host. All friendship is based on trust; sooner or later your tendency to opt for the better offer will be discovered and you'll be discredited. Once you've accepted an invitation, nothing short of serious illness ought to stop you honouring that commitment. And try to derive consolation from the thought that no matter how great the other occasion promises to be, it'll now suffer from one fatal drawback – your absence.

What to do if you went ahead, cancelled the old college pals and accepted dinner with Jude Law? Your double-dealing ways have now been discovered and the pals are seriously offended – as is their right? No further dissembling please. Confess the error of your ways at once, humbly beg everyone's pardon and give assurances that you'll never, ever behave in the same way again. Don't even think about criticizing the event you did attend. ('Actually, Jude Law was really dull and I wish I'd had supper with you lot instead.') That kind of attitude will only compound your difficulties and probably cause further offence to one or both parties.

After apologizing, you still mightn't be asked around again by the old college pals, but at least they'll feel more kindly towards you than would otherwise be the case.

LEARNING TO SAY NO

Luckily for every guest, certain hosts are consistently, extravagantly, ludicrously hospitable. They ask you back time and again, forever suggesting you drop in for drinks, remain for a kitchen supper, stay the entire weekend. Basically they do everything except suggest that you move in permanently with them.

Sometimes, though, it's better to turn down their invitations, no matter how attractive or gratifying these might appear. Treat yourself as the social equivalent of rich chocolate: to be enjoyed only in small and carefully measured quantities. Or think of yourself as currency: the less of you that's in circulation, the more you're worth on any specific occasion. Don't devalue your worth by being always available.

Learn how to say no, without panicking that a refusal to attend another party will:

- Cause your hosts grave offence leading to …
- Their withdrawal of all future invitations resulting in …
- Your becoming society's pariah and …
- Forever after leading a lonely and tragic existence in which your only company is a family of flea-infested cats.

Before reaching this pitiful conclusion and adopting a litter of kittens, appreciate that if you're thought good enough to be asked once, you'll remain good enough to be asked a second time. And when you accept the second invitation, your presence will be all the more appreciated because of its relative rarity.

How to Win a Reputation for Being a Good Guest

PUNCTUALITY

Here is a conundrum: to turn up precisely on time, or not to turn up precisely on time? That's the question puzzling so many

— Hi, Sorry we're late!

guests. Whether it's nobler to be punctual and suffer sitting alone for half an hour in the living-room (while your hosts dash about frantically trying to get themselves, and the rest of the house, in a fit state to receive you), or whether it's more sensible to arrive twenty minutes or so after the appointed time, confident that by then the party should have got properly underway.

Because absolute rules no longer apply, you're better to resolve any uncertainty in advance. When, for example, an invitation arrives requesting your presence at eight for eight-thirty, what precisely does this mean? Perhaps you're expected to turn up on the dot of the earlier time in order to be marshalled into dinner at the later. Or maybe you shouldn't think of arriving before half-eight unless you enjoy the illicit thrill of seeing your hostess wrapped up in a bath towel. Stop dithering and just call your hosts: they'll be only too happy to give you a precise time of arrival.

Having been informed of that, it's absolutely imperative you obey instructions. Lack of punctuality is one of the clearest signs of profound selfishness, evidence that you believe yourself – and your erratic time-keeping – to be more important than anyone else, including your host. No one should have to sit in a restaurant or living-room waiting for your arrival because you didn't check the route beforehand and are now lost in a maze of suburban cul-de-sacs. Likewise, a carefully planned dinner shouldn't be ruined because you're still at home unable to decide which dress to wear.

'Punctuality', said Louis xviii, 'is the politeness of kings.' If it's good enough for royalty, it's good enough for you. Learn how to be on time and, should you be running late, at least have the good manners to let your hosts or friends know as soon as possible. Don't rely on telepathy as a means of communicating this information; it has consistently proven to be as undependable as you are.

Most sensibly of all, set off a little earlier than is really necessary; that way, you'll arrive calm and composed, instead of perspiring and apologetic.

By the way, parents of small children: you're allowed to use the line about the baby-sitter turning up late just once. It mustn't become a regular part of your script.

NERVES

Everyone, whether host or guest, feels at least a little nervous before, and even during, a party. Once you acknowledge this truism, already the feeling isn't so bad anymore because it has become communal rather than specific to you.

The trick is to channel energy produced by nervousness in a positive fashion – use it to your advantage instead of letting social apprehension stifle you. If you're worried about having nothing to say, run through a couple of possible conversation topics in advance. This doesn't mean you need to have entire speeches prepared in advance ('and the third law of thermodynamics is …' while an expression of glazed indifference forms on everyone else's faces). It simply guarantees you arrive at a party with something to say for yourself. Read the morning's paper, it should provide you with an abundance of potential subject matter.

If this seems too demanding, learn to ask other guests questions. Make these more of the 'So what do you do?' variety, rather than the 'Is there really an afterlife and if so what form does it take?' type. It remains regrettably true that, for all of us, the subject on which we speak with most gusto is ourselves. Encourage other people to do the talking and you'll quickly gain a reputation of being intelligent and perceptive.

Resist the temptation to discuss how nervous you feel. Either the conversation will end up taking a turn for the competitive (i.e. 'I'm much more socially timid than you'll ever be') or else you'll be looked upon as a freak.

Also avoid the seemingly attractive option of taking a few drinks to ease your nerves. Having finally toppled over in a drunken stupor, you'll be comatose, not calm.

All social life is meant to be a pleasure rather than a penance. Whenever it feels more like the latter than the former, you should reconsider accepting certain invitations because your discomfort risks transmitting itself to other guests and will do nothing to enhance your general popularity. If large crowds intimidate you, avoid those kind of parties. Likewise, skip dinners should the thought of a long night conversing with just a few people bring you out in a panicky sweat. Only attend events where you're confident of feeling your most relaxed. That should go a long way to reducing your nervousness.

By the way, a constant mystery on the social circuit is that the parties you most look forward to invariably fall a little flat, whereas those you dread often turn out to be rather fun. So maybe a few pre-party nerves aren't a bad thing.

ALLERGIES

Don't eat peanuts? Won't eat Brussels sprouts? No problem, provided you give enough notice. There are few more annoying surprises than the guest who only announces food allergies as dinner is being served. Should you have a problem with certain foods warn your hosts well in advance. No doubt every effort will be made to accommodate your particular needs.

What if you forgot to tell your hosts about your specific dietary requirements and are now faced with a plate of (to you, at least) inedible shellfish? Don't make a fuss and don't draw attention to yourself. The rest of the party really doesn't need to hear about your difficulties with suspected irritable bowel syndrome or the time you were rushed to hospital after accidentally tasting a morsel of fresh mayonnaise. ('I can't even be in the same room as a raw egg.')

If anyone draws attention to your lacklustre appetite, offer an apologetic excuse – you ate an enormous lunch or you've a ridiculously sweet tooth and are waiting for the last course – and then change the subject as quickly as possible.

Similarly, if you've any other allergies – feather pillows, pets, small children – always state them when accepting an invitation, but make a point of insisting that no special arrangements should be made for you. Hosts are already harassed enough without having to draw up a separate menu or arranging to kennel their dog just to keep you happy. The good guest learns how to adapt to circumstances.

And if you're one of those people with a long list of special needs? Well, maybe it's better that you turn down social engagements and stay put in your own dust-, child- and nut-free environment.

ENTERTAINMENT

You play the piano divinely. You're a brilliant juggler. You've an extensive repertoire of show tunes. You studied magic for five years and can perform complicated card tricks. Good for you. But keep any/all of the above skills to yourself unless invited by your hosts to demonstrate them.

The urge to show off in company is a powerful one. Nevertheless, it needs to be suppressed because the evening's original plans almost certainly didn't include you demonstrating the strength of your vocal chords or your ability to remember a long and complicated joke. There's an enormous difference between how we perceive ourselves and how others see us. We might fondly imagine that wherever two or more are gathered together, our ability to tell a funny story will always receive a warm welcome. In reality, the welcome is, at best, cool.

On the other hand, if your hosts do ask you to perform (preferably with sufficient advance warning that you can rehearse or at least prepare yourself), agree to do so. Unless you're Frank Sinatra reincarnated, keep your performance short, try to make it funny and firmly refuse all demands for an encore. Skilled performers learn it's best to leave an audience wanting more.

Should other guests be invited to show off their own party piece, have the good manners not to talk through their recitation of the Beowulf saga/Bartók song cycle/knife juggling routine. Stifle all yawns, look impressed at this demonstration of talent – and have a full glass of whatever you fancy close at hand to keep you going.

Sometimes your hosts will have arranged entertainment at a party. This is a nuisance because invariably it begins just as you've become engrossed in a really good chat with someone else. The performance could be the hosts' children playing on violin and triangle (shades of *The Sound of Music* and an old set of curtains being put to good use). Or it could be a professional actor pretending to be a Drunken Guest – although the latter has always seemed a bit mystifying, when plenty of real guests are able to play this role with aplomb. Whatever the choice, once again give the impression of being thrilled by the spectacle and make sure you make mention of it when saying your goodbyes (this will occur shortly after the third encore of violin and triangle).

KITCHEN DUTIES

Go into the kitchen only if you're prepared to help – but do be prepared for your offer to be turned down. If this occurs, leave immediately; you'll only get in the way, because even professional chefs on television never seem to have enough space and end up shouting abuse at some innocent who's blocking access to the blender. Should hosts accept your offer of assistance, it's highly unlikely the task will involve cooking the meal – by now, they'll have worked out what needs to be done by themselves. Save the demonstration of your fantastic culinary skills for whenever you return their hospitality.

Your role in someone else's kitchen will be a fairly menial one – anything from dicing vegetables to scrubbing a saucepan; the best you can hope for is a request to mix the salad dressing. Contemporary kitchens are usually quite small, so cleaning up before/during/after cooking is a constant necessity and your assistance here could be invaluable. Rather than criticize its abilities to remove all residue, you might propose loading the dishwasher, for example, or giving the wine glasses a polish before dinner. Find ways to make yourself useful but if these involve making too many demands on busy hosts (of the 'Where do you keep your napkins?' or 'What's that used for?' kind) it might be best to leave things to others better qualified.

OVER-FAMILIARITY

No matter how long or how well you know your hosts, nor how often they've entertained you, the indisputable fact is that you're a guest and you retain certain obligations. The most important of these is to be adequately grateful each and every time you enjoy hospitality. Imagine that one of your neighbours has given you a lift to work each morning for the past decade; the length of time doesn't transform this act of generosity into your entitlement. The same is also true of hospitality; presume it's a right and not a privilege and you risk having it removed. Hosts can, quite understandably, develop powerful grudges against a guest who forgets to say thank you, or worse, comes to believe it isn't necessary to do so any more.

Always retain a certain formality, albeit of the barely visible sort. Without first asking permission, you're not allowed to refill your wineglass, help yourself to food from the fridge, switch on the television or play a CD on the music system. This way no one can ever accuse you of overstepping a boundary you didn't know existed. This way too, you're much more likely to avoid one of those sudden rows that can explode after you've done something seemingly innocent, like thrown your feet up on a friend's sofa. You've been doing the same thing for years; only now has it become an issue. Remember: somebody else's home can never be your own – no matter how often you're asked to treat it as such.

BREAKING AND BORROWING

All guests are prone to both of these, and both run the risk of causing their hosts serious aggravation. If you break/damage anything that isn't your own, tell the owners at once, or as soon as you possibly can. Be contrite and offer to replace the item in question or pay for its repair. A good host will immediately respond that this isn't necessary; Granny's priceless Meissen dinner service was really very impractical and by breaking several pieces you've provided the spur to buy a set of sensible dishwasher-proof plates. Override these polite platitudes with your own insistence. You smashed the Meissen, you've now got to replace it. That's an absolute rule for all guests.

Borrowing: You must always ask first. Making a 'they won't mind/won't miss it' argument to yourself isn't the point. That book or CD or scarf or sum of money doesn't belong to you. Therefore you have to be given permission before borrowing it.

Don't take umbrage if your hosts ask you to write them a little 'borrowed by …' note. This doesn't mean they don't trust your honesty, merely that they don't trust their own memories. Of course, if they stamp the inside cover of the book with a return-by date and warn you about fines charged for lateness, maybe it's better not to borrow from them.

Prompt returns, though, are important. Make sure the book you were loaned isn't still sitting on your shelves three years later. Return it a.s.a.p. – and preferably accompanied by a letter of thanks.

LEAVING

When it comes to exits, there are the good, the bad and the downright messy. Make sure your departure from any social gathering is as well timed as your arrival. The simplest rule to memorize is this: never be the last person to go. That's applicable no matter how much your hosts press you to stay. The most important thing to leave behind is a longing for more of your company; this is unlikely to occur if you're still holding court in someone else's house at six in the morning. So, once you see other guests preparing to move on, make your own preparations to follow suit.

At a big party you don't need to say goodbye to everyone, but if someone in the midst of a tête-à-tête catches your eye as you're heading out the door, wave or signal your goodbye without causing any disruption.

Insist your hosts don't accompany you to the door; they'll probably ignore your pleas but you should try. The only exception to the above advice is when you're at a big party, the hosts are at the far end of the room and it would be incredibly disruptive to demand their attention. In which case, simply slip away.

THANK YOUS

Saying thank you for hospitality is important and the best way to do this is in writing. A good handwritten thank-you letter will always endear you to your hosts.

When writing to thank your hosts, try to be specific rather than general in your remarks. After a lunch or dinner party, for example, instead of just saying how much you loved the food, pick out one dish for particular mention. Was there a topic of conversation that caught everyone's attention or another guest whose company you really enjoyed? If so, be sure to comment on these details in your letter, because that will show how memorable you found the occasion. Above all, be prompt. Try to write your letter the following day and definitely don't allow more than a week to pass before sending it. The longer you leave this task, the less fresh will be your enthusiasm and, very likely, the more bland your appreciation.

What about using the telephone for your thank yous or newer technology such as emails and text messages? A lot depends on the circumstances – and probably also on the age of your hosts. Despite the internet becoming more widespread a surprisingly large number of people still don't understand it or prefer to use it only for work purposes.

Other Useful Points for Guests

GATE-CRASHING
Over the age of eighteen, gate-crashing is inexcusable behaviour. You shouldn't do it – and if you do, prepare for the possibility of being asked to leave. When this happens, don't dispute your putative hosts' rights, just go.

UNWANTED ATTENTIONS
The knee that presses a little too fervently against your own. The hand that wanders across an expanse of sofa to entwine itself around your shoulders. The foot that strays under the table and is now meandering up and down your leg. Flattering perhaps, but unwanted certainly. Something must be done.

What form the 'something' takes will depend on who's paying you the attention, and on its form. If the person is another guest, make your lack of interest apparent as speedily as possible. Some people still believe that the word 'no' is really a coded means of saying yes.

Remove the unwanted hand – or whatever anatomical part is causing you trouble – and speak your mind plainly, firmly but quietly. Then move yourself as far out of range as you can. It's terribly tempting under these circumstances to make a public spectacle of the pest, but being unkind only compounds the problem. Besides, there could be reasons unknown to you why you've been singled out for this unsolicited notice – aside from your being extraordinarily gorgeous and sensual, of course. The person responsible might be drunk/tired/going through an emotional crisis/on medication and acting out of character. Noisy denunciations serve no purpose except to cause general embarrassment. Presumably that's not your intention. But you might want to tell your hosts about the incident, either at once or later. Then they can make sure it doesn't happen again to a guest in their house.

More problematic are those occasions when the person pestering you is your host. Most of us will have been invited to dinner and belatedly realized we were supposed to be the last course on the night's menu. If this turns out to be the case – your host's hands turn exploratory and there are no other guests around – you're entitled to make your apologies and leave.

The presence of fellow guests should spare you the worst; just make sure you're among the first of the party's departures. Ring or write your customary thanks without alluding to any incident that might have taken place and turn down invitations from that particular host for the next six months or however much time you think advisable.

Most pests are harmless and easily swatted off; their efforts to ensnare you will make an amusing story later. But occasionally they're much more troublesome and even dangerous. If you find yourself the recipient of persistent unwanted attention from someone who attempts to force you to do something without your complete consent, immediately report the incident to the relevant official authorities. You've an obligation to do this, both to yourself and to others who at some future date could find themselves in a similar situation.

CARNAL URGES

It's best to leave your libido at home when you're being entertained by someone else as a certain degree of decorum is expected on most social occasions. Guests only have a handful of obligations and chief among them is the duty to be sociable. There's something tiresome – and adolescent – about couples who spend an entire party pawing one another. If you really don't want to communicate with anybody other than your current partner, why not stay at home together? Intermittent handholding is fine, anything more demonstrative risks excluding you from the rest of the company.

If you should meet someone extremely attractive for the first time at a party, avoid the urge to consummate your relationship on the premises. Instead, arrange to meet again soon when the two of you can be alone. But (without going into too much specific detail, of course) tell your hosts later about this unexpected outcome of their party. Everyone likes to be thought a successful matchmaker.

SHYNESS

In a child, shyness is absolutely delightful and certainly much more appealing than precociousness, which now seems to be the only alternative option. But once you have left behind childhood, you should also relinquish any claims to being shy.

Still feeling hopelessly self-effacing? You're not alone. Everybody suffers from varying degrees of the condition. Make it your mantra that you aren't alone and things won't seem so bad. But you shouldn't let it hinder your social life. Learn which occasions induce the worst outbreaks of shyness and avoid them as much as possible. You're likely to find that drinks parties are especially difficult.

But shyness can also be a form of selfishness; you're so busy thinking about one particular person – namely yourself – that everyone else becomes rather unimportant. And from the outside, adult shyness often appears just plain rude. While you might like to console yourself by imagining that at least you look mysterious and brooding, the rest of the room's more likely to see someone who won't join in the conversation and prefers to give the impression of being bored and aloof.

Also, watch out for other people's shyness at a party and see what you can do to help. There's no need to sign up to the Samaritans before you go out for the night. Just remember the many times when you'd have appreciated interest from a fellow guest. Shyness might be childish but not all of us can be grown-up all of the time.

TABLE MANNERS (AND THE LIKE)
Never put your elbows on the table. Talk to the person seated on one side of you for the first course and whoever is on the other during the next. Work your way through the cutlery starting with the piece furthest from the centre. Phooey to all that. You could allow yourself to be governed by these old-fashioned rules or you could accept that manners at table – just like those everywhere else – are primarily concerned with showing courtesy and consideration to others.

Should you know the basic rules of traditional behaviour at table and the person next to you doesn't – he's just poured wine into the water glass, for example, used a dessert fork to eat the first course or treated the napkin as a handkerchief – ought you to say anything? That depends on the individual concerned; if he appears uncomfortable or uncertain about what to do, yes, step in to offer help and guidance. But really these social faux pas matter very little; better your neighbour uses the wrong fork than not eat at all.

Meanwhile, there are lots of other ways you can provide a demonstration of your own perfect manners. Distracted hosts, rushing around trying to cook and present the food, can sometimes fail to spot that one of their guests has been left with no one to talk to. If you see this, be inclusive and draw the person into your conversation; there are few more socially mortifying experiences than being left staring at the dinner table because no one can be bothered to speak to you.

Have the guests in your vicinity got everything they need? Did the bowl of salad pass them by? Would their wineglass benefit from being topped up? Are they missing some essential implement? If so, see what you can do to help before tucking into your own plate and your thoughtfulness will be appreciated by guest and hosts alike. Likewise, if there's an accident act to resolve the problem speedily and with as little drama as possible. While performing an emergency tracheotomy on a choking neighbour at table might test your skills, you should be able to resolve most other difficulties without disturbing the rest of the party.

Talk Is Cheap (But It Can Cost You Dear)

GOSSIP

Be honest: we all do it. We all claim not to do so, but we do. So let's have no pretence that things are otherwise. The following points should also be agreed:

- No gossiping about your hosts. Ideally, that means no gossiping about anyone whose hospitality you've enjoyed – ever. However, we live in the real world, not an ideal one, so let's settle for the feasible. The one absolute and unbreakable rule: gossiping about your hosts isn't permitted while in their company. They're going through a rough marital patch? She's just lost her job? He's hitting the bottle a bit hard? That's tough enough without catching a knot of guests having a whispered discussion on the subject. Gossiping about hosts is intensely disloyal to the people who've asked you into their home. Discover someone else trying to initiate such a conversation? You're not just entitled, you're obliged to put a stop to it right away.
- Ditto about other guests; you really shouldn't be sunk on the sofa pondering whether that couple at the other end of the room, each married to someone else, is having an affair. Keep any thoughts on the subject strictly to yourself.
- There's bad gossip and there's not-so-bad gossip and, occa-

sionally, there's even good gossip. The first involves repeating titbits that oughtn't, under any circumstances, to be repeated. Why do you feel the need to tell one friend what another said about her over lunch yesterday if it was unkind/unpleasant? You could try loftily justifying your behaviour by saying the second friend deserved or had a right to know what was being said about her. But did she? Or was it just that you enjoyed watching her discomfort and this gave you a certain satisfaction? If so, how would you feel were roles reversed and it was you hearing repeated what a third party had said about your personal hygiene/table manners/sexual habits? No good comes from spreading bad news because everybody – including the messenger – ends up being tainted. People who make a habit of passing on unpleasant gossip are best avoided.

- Always repeat good gossip as fast as possible. Hand on compliments or kind thoughts to the person who was discussed.

COMPLAINING

Complaining takes three forms:

- *Addressed to the host:* Never draw your hosts' attention to their inadequacies unless failure to do so could result in a serious health hazard. The sheets are damp, for example, and you've barely recovered from pneumonia, or the chicken about to be served is undercooked and will give everyone at the table food poisoning. Concern for people other than yourself obliges you to point out a problem. Do so quietly and tactfully, if possible without drawing anyone else's attention to the matter.

- *Addressed to other guests:* Obviously it's best not to give vent to a 'you-know-I-hate-cheese' whinge in front of either your hosts or other guests. But some of the latter can be tempted to kvetch. You'll discover them comfortably ensconced in someone else's home, moaning about the décor, the canapés, the quality of wine being served. Shame on them – and on you if your voice is ever heard among their number.

↝ *Addressed to friends after the event*: Don't imagine it's permissible to carry your complaints elsewhere. 'She always puts me sitting next to the dullest people,' you groan to friends about last night's hostess, or, 'The main course was completely inedible; why do they bother trying to cook?' Like the song says, accentuate the positive. Even if the food really was vile, the wine no better than dishwater, the company so boring that you had trouble staying awake beyond nine o'clock, there must have been something to praise about the event. Mustn't there? And if the answer's still no, then don't accept any more invitations from that host.

VERBAL FAUX PAS

No matter how polite, well mannered or considerate we might be, the probability of sooner or later making a faux pas remains high.

There are several reasons why they occur, the first of which is plain ignorance: how were you to know that the subject of your scorn was about to walk into the room or that puréed turnip was the highlight of this evening's menu? But just as often we're prone to being carried away either through nervousness or, quite the reverse, excessive self-confidence. Then we speak out of turn and cause offence.

Whenever something you've said gets an unexpectedly hostile reaction, find out what's wrong and, if necessary, apologize. Don't make matters worse by trying to joke about what's happened or blustering that people shouldn't be so thin-skinned.

You witness someone else's faux pas? See what, if anything, you can do to smooth matters over quickly. Once the error has been recognized and apologies have been made and – ideally –

accepted, help the awkwardness to pass by introducing another topic of conversation.

XENOPHOBIA (AND OTHER OUTBREAKS OF NASTINESS)

Conversation is flowing comfortably round the dinner table when, without warning, someone makes an unpleasantly racist/ sexist/homophobic/ageist remark. That someone could even be the host whose company you'd been enjoying until now. What to do?

Immediately, try working out whether the remark was flippant or serious, whether intended merely for effect – however unpleasant – or the expression of deeply held beliefs that are contrary to your own. As a rule, when faced with a quiet challenge, comments of this kind are quickly withdrawn.

But what also needs to be judged is the importance of the subject to you and how far you're therefore prepared to go. Does another guest's advocacy of fox-hunting, for example, merit disrupting the rest of the dinner table?

If your answer is yes, then understand from the start what you're doing and the potential consequences. Keep your counsel or argue your case firmly, calmly and cogently. Don't shout and don't become angry – both will damage your argument. Bear in mind that this is a dinner table, not a debating society.

Finally, you have to decide which matters more: your social life or your personal beliefs. The second ought to take precedence, although don't forget that your own temperament (or too much alcohol) could have led you to exaggerate the significance of whatever has been said by another guest. But if it really has upset you and affected your attitude to the party, the only option remaining is to explain your feelings to the host and leave. You mightn't be asked back, but then again, would you want to spend any more time in that sort of company?

BAD LANGUAGE

Can easily be summarized as follows: don't use it; don't be shocked if other people do.

Swear words debase all language, particularly when they occur in profusion. Repetition has devalued swearing in our society to the point that it no longer has much impact. Nevertheless, an older generation – whether your hosts, your fellow guests, or yourself – can still find its use offensive and distasteful. You've an obligation to consider the feelings of others, no matter how different they are from your own. While you might swear with gusto when alone, curb the habit in company.

Equally important: erase from your speech any language that might be thought blasphemous to the religious-minded. Some words and terms have become so commonplace that we use them unthinkingly, but they could be offensive to others.

VERBOSITY

An old maxim says that empty vessels make the most noise. Remember it. Talking too much can have the effect of making you appear vainglorious and of infuriating everyone else.

There's a considerable difference between a conversation and a monologue; the first involves a number of people, the second only one.

Under no circumstances begin a sentence with the words, 'This'll amuse you.' It's practically throwing down the gauntlet to everyone else in the room that they're not allowed to remain stony-faced while you're speaking. Or that they're now obliged to do their not-so-best to stifle successive yawns.

Guests who've been told they're funny are particularly prone to attacks of verbosity, as are members of certain professions such as law where speech-making's the norm. Should you be a successful barrister, save your twenty-minute talks for the courtroom; at a drinks party, they'll have you quickly certified as a bore. Unless you want to become the ancient mariner of the social circuit, skip all yarn telling.

Allow other people to speak – and not merely to remark how funny you are before you launch into your next story. Still vulnerable to verbosity? Give the job of bore monitor to your partner/spouse. Many of them take on the task unofficially; at every party, there's always at least one couple tetchily having a 'Darling, I'm sure nobody wants to hear that story again' exchange.

2. Being a Good Host

S ome people, no matter how hard they try, never manage to throw a decent party. What's often most frustrating for these thwarted hosts is that they've taken so much trouble to get everything right whereas someone else who has casually asked a few friends around is universally hailed as the Host with the Most. This chapter offers some advice to would-be hosts.

Throwing a Party

Top tips: Whether it's a formal dinner or Friday evening post-work drinks, don't be afraid to over-invite. Without doubt, at least one, if not more, of your guests will cancel at the last minute. Nobody minds a bit of a social squeeze. It's better than a handful of guests gazing at one another across acres of emptiness.

Get the mix right. Always invite one or two new people to your party, rather than just see the same group of old friends.

Worried that you won't have everything ready in time or will forget something vital? Make a list.

Lists are invaluable – have one hanging in a convenient place in your kitchen and keep a pen close to hand so that you can tick off each task as it's accomplished. That way, your party should run as smoothly as you'd like.

Still feeling nervous? Ask some good friends to come around early and give a hand with last-minute preparations (such as putting out olives in little bowls while you go for a quick bath and a drink). Invariably, despite your meticulous list, you'll still have forgotten something – like the dry-cleaning tag on the back of your dress or a fresh loo roll in the bathroom. Your friends will spot these faster than you.

The other advantage to an early appearance by the good friends is that when the first 'real' guests arrive – and of course, without fail, they'll be a couple you hardly know and only invited because their three-year-old goes to the same school as your own little darling – there's already someone else present to help with the initial awkward-conversation phase.

The Drinks Party

A drinks party doesn't mean inviting a few friends to hang around the house drinking beer and watching the afternoon's soccer on your plasma-screen television. The drinks party can be clearly identified by the following key features:

- The event takes place within clearly prescribed hours. Drink is the primary refreshment offered, although sometimes small items of food stabbed onto wooden sticks are passed around.
- Everyone present stands – except for one overweight guest who'll threaten the future of your favourite chair by perching precariously on its arm.
- For the first half-hour, guests look – and feel – deeply uncomfortable and struggle to find something to say to one another.
- The party then assumes a frenzied atmosphere as too many

people are compressed into too small a space, all of them trying to say too much too loudly. You, the host, will spend this part of the evening attempting, without success, to make your way from one end of the room to the other. Old friends will come and go without ever seeing or speaking to you.

- Guests now begin to leave and you're finally able to enjoy yourself because oxygen can circulate around the room again and so can you.
- You will have trouble getting rid of any guest who's made no plans to do something after the party's prescribed time ends.

Don't make a move on somebody at your own party. Even if you know his marriage is going through a rough patch, this won't be a good moment to tell your neighbour about the crush you've had on him for the past five years. You'll have too many other distractions and demands being made on your time. Focus all the attention on one individual and you'll probably end up neglecting other guests. Certainly, invite a potential lover to your party, but only so that he or she can see what a great home/set of friends/social life you have.

Only host a drinks party if you've arranged to do something or go somewhere afterwards. Otherwise your guests will ignore the clearly prescribed hours and still be looking for more drink at three o'clock in the morning. Make a dinner reservation at a local restaurant and inform everyone of this in advance. You might like to suggest that guests join you for a meal afterwards, strictly on a pay-your-own-way basis, of course. Alternatively, plan to host your drinks party on a night when you've already been invited to dinner in another house. That way, you've a cast-iron excuse for evicting guests from your home by a certain time.

You'd rather not go out to dinner, either alone or with anyone else? Nevertheless, claim that this is your intention. If necessary, be prepared to put on your coat, leave the house and walk around the block a couple of times. Sometimes, desperate measures are needed to clear out the residual guests.

PREPARATION
Before your drinks party, hide all breakables. Small items of sentimental or monetary value should not be left exposed on open surfaces. Your friends aren't thieves but they can be clumsy, especially in a crowded room and after alcohol's been consumed. If you want your collection of porcelain figurines representing the entire cast of *EastEnders* to survive the night intact, put them away. Otherwise, should breakages occur, you've no one to blame but yourself.

Also, prior to the first guests' arrival, even if nobody you've invited is a smoker, place an ashtray on every surface in the room – all table tops, window sills, above the fireplace, etc. After consuming a certain amount of alcohol – the quantity can vary from two glasses to two bottles – at least one confirmed non-smoker will develop an irresistible craving for nicotine and light a cigarette. This, by the way, will have been cadged from another confirmed non-smoker, and suddenly your living-room is dense with people nonchalantly waving cigarettes about. With every wave, they will sprinkle some ash. You'll still find a couple of butts trampled into your oak floor or expensive Persian kilim but far fewer than would otherwise be the case.

Are you entitled to forbid smoking in your home? Yes, you are. Will this interdiction be appreciated? No, it won't. Nor will it necessarily be obeyed; at some point in the evening, you'll come across a group of smokers huddled together in the bathroom or kitchen. Working on the principle that there's strength in numbers, they'll have defied your smoking ban.

ASK A TEENAGER TO PASS ROUND THE DRINKS

HELP

You can't expect to look after everyone single-handedly. Can you afford to hire help? Not necessarily a professional (and expensive) waiter, but maybe a nephew/niece looking to earn a little cash. Or a student who's short of funds. Young children often love this kind of work because it makes them feel grown-up. Just make sure your amateur help, especially if under-age, doesn't see helping as an opportunity to consume as much alcohol as he/she serves. Because the range of drinks you'll be offering is quite small and simple (see below), the job of temporary barman should be easy. It's primarily a question of pouring and clearing.

If you've no young relatives to help out or can't run to the cost of paying an impoverished student, ask loyal friends to come early and give you a hand with the serving. Present each of them with a bottle or jug to take around the room and top up glasses. The thoughtful friend will also use this opportunity to collect any empties and return them to the kitchen. Nobody's more popular at a drinks party than the person holding a full bottle, so this a great way to make new acquaintances.

INTRODUCTIONS

These must be performed, especially at the beginning of the party when there are just a handful of people in the room. Later, when the place is jammed – and even you don't know half the people present – it's permissible to let guests take responsibility for introducing themselves. But do keep an eye open for Susan Self-Effacing, who's hovering at the periphery of the party, like someone standing on a wintry seashore unwilling to rush into the water. She'll need a helping hand and, if it's done well, you'll later have the satisfaction of seeing her happily splashing about in the social tide.

Worried about making introductions in a crowded room? Once again, before the party starts ask a self-confident friend or two to help with this task. The busy host is always allowed to delegate.

How to perform introductions? Traditionally, you're supposed to introduce a man to a woman and a younger person to an older. The majority of hosts, though, are already so fraught that they just introduce in any fashion. What matters most is that you state everyone's name clearly and loudly enough for these to be heard. In other words, say, 'Have you met Susan Self-Effacing? Sue, this is Aileen Assured.' Otherwise, Susan and Aileen will have to go through the 'Sorry, what's your name again?' routine. Ideally first names and surnames should both be given, but if this seems to be too much, the first will do. Remember that just because a woman is married, this no longer means she wants to be introduced with her husband's surname.

And don't introduce people by their private nicknames.

Multiple introductions – when poor Susan is led up like a sacrificial lamb to meet six other people simultaneously – should be avoided. Their happy chatter will stop, she'll be embarrassed at becoming the object of everyone else's attention and will certainly not remember one, let alone six, new names. Ease Susan into the group by introducing her only to whoever's nearest and then, ideally, she'll be absorbed into the collective conversation.

It's also incredibly helpful when introducing Susan to Aileen if you can provide each of them with some small nugget of information about the other. Obviously, the nugget shouldn't be a *non sequitur*. Announcing that Aileen plays tennis every afternoon will be of no help to Susan if the latter's extremely non-sporty. What you're looking for is an area of common interest that can act as the starting point for a conversation. This can be anything from, 'Aileen also got lost on her way here tonight,' to 'Don't your children go to the same school?' Hover briefly to see that the two women have taken the bait and are chatting away, and then move on. Keep mingling. The one person who is never going to have an opportunity for a decent chat at your party will be you.

Note to guests: Learn to introduce yourselves. Walk towards someone else, extend your hand, state your name, ask what the other person is called and then have ready a remark that can act as a conversational opening gambit such as, 'Did you get lost on your way here as well?' or 'Aren't your children in the same school as our two?'

Guests who do this are greatly valued by hosts.

SUGGESTED DRINKS
What to serve at your drinks party? Unless you've hired lots of bar staff or enjoy the sense of being under pressure, keep things

simple. Limit what you provide to just a handful of items but have a lot of these in stock: the primary requirement of a drinks party is that there's enough drink.

One of your guests brings a bottle to the party? Even if better than whatever you're serving, put the present away for drinking later. Some things to consider:

- *Champagne:* It's delicious, and immediately establishes a festive atmosphere. But it's also expensive and will probably be outside your price range if you've invited more than a handful of people. There's a way around this problem, which is to serve a sparkling wine instead of champagne. Almost every wine-producing country produces its own version of champagne and a lot of them taste fine. Unfortunately, though, not quite as fine as the original – which is why non-champagnes are quite a lot cheaper. How to disguise this fact? Mix the sparkling wine with something else such as orange juice. Alternative, and better, options include fresh peach or strawberry juice (both made by pulping plenty of the appropriate fruit). Mix this with the sparkling wine in a large jug. Serve in fluted glasses decorated with a tiny sliver of fruit and your guests will be delighted.

- *A cocktail:* But make it something simple like a Sea Breeze. (One third each of grapefruit juice, cranberry juice and vodka. Mix together in a jug, add ice and pour.) You don't want to spend the night rattling up a cocktail shaker and blending together obscure ingredients like white chartreuse that can only be found in one shop somewhere in the Swiss Alps. Pick a drink that's vodka-based and primarily involves the addition of just a couple of other ingredients – including fruit juice because that will dilute both the alcohol content and your eventual bill. Mix everything together in a jug and pour into tumblers containing ice (again, this helps to make the drink stretch further).

In the summer (or any day that approximates to this), think of serving Pimms, which is incredibly easy to make and fantastically refreshing. This involves taking a large jug and cramming it with an abundance of orange, lemon, lime and apple slices, plus a lot of fresh mint leaves and some ice cubes. Then fill one-third of whatever space is left in the jug with Pimms and the remaining two-thirds with cold lemonade (you might like to replace some of the lemonade with a generous slug of gin). Thanks to all the pieces of fruit stuffed in every glass, Pimms works out quite economically – and you can even claim that the citrus content makes it a healthy drink.

- *Wine:* Offer both red and white. Make sure the second of these is adequately chilled – and if you've a few bottles of fizzy water, spritzers can be offered to guests as well (another budget-stretching device). Buy your wine by the case. Every retailer now provides a sale-or-return service so what's not consumed can be brought back to the shop afterwards. The wine you serve at a drinks party should remain consistent and not change vineyards, vintages or continents between one glass and the next.

  It's worth pointing out that wine can actually prove an expensive choice for your party because what's served has to be palatable enough to drink on its own and without the masking help of food. Good wine is not cheap. Nevertheless, no plonk please.

- *Non-alcoholic drinks:* Some of your guests – often more than you expect – will only want something 'soft' to drink. Perhaps they're designated drivers or are on some kind of diet or just don't touch alcohol at all. Please, make an effort for them. Too often, all the nicest drink is reserved for the alcoholic element of the party and the only other offering is tap water. There are alternatives: how about mixing up a delicious fruit punch, for example, free of alcohol but crammed full of flavour? Teetotallers are frequently treated in the same off-hand manner as vegetarians and expected to be happy with the liquid equivalent of a plain omelette.

FOOD

Is a bonus and not a fundamental requirement. Only provide whatever's within your capabilities and your budget. You should be able to afford a few bowls of nuts or olives. Remember, though, that the high-salt content of these will stimulate thirst, leading to further requests for drink from your guests.

Canapés? Thanks very much but again, bear in mind that they'll demand your attention. Even if bought ready-made, canapés still have to be laid out on plates beforehand, probably during that valuable twenty minutes you'd set aside for a bath.

HOW TO GET RID OF AN OLIVE STONE

They might have to be heated in the oven (and only heated, not burnt to a crisp because you forgot about them while organizing drinks for guests who'd just walked in). Someone will have to hand around the canapés. That someone will most probably be you because the friends invited early to give you a helping hand are now happily engrossed in conversation elsewhere. And the canapés will need to be accompanied by small paper napkins, otherwise when the party's over you'll find greasy fingermarks on your new curtains (without fail, canapés have a high-fat content).

You will, in any case, later find folded napkins tucked down the side of armchairs, inside flowerpots and behind photograph frames. Set out dishes for soiled paper napkins. The same receptacles will also be useful for holding unswallowed olive stones and cocktail sticks. At least one guest will not take the trouble to drop the sticks into the dish provided for this purpose, preferring instead to stuff them behind a cushion where several napkins have already been concealed.

Only masochists and the handful of people rich enough to afford caterers serve home-made canapés. They're tiny, fiddly things that take hours to make and microseconds to consume. Guests will be so busy chatting to each other that they won't pay any attention to your culinary efforts. At a drinks party, food is like blotting paper; its sole function is to soak up alcohol. If you want to serve canapés, buy them prepared. What you spend in extra funds, you'll save in extra time.

The Dinner Party

A successful dinner party depends on good planning, so this is definitely an occasion for list-making. You'll want to make an overall plan of campaign that includes the following headings:

Guests
Menu
Shopping
Countdown to the meal
Table plan

GUESTS

Work out who you'd like to have on your perfect guest wish list – and then add a few extra names to this, without fail not everyone's going to accept and in any case how many people can you comfortably fit around the table? Eight, but ten at a squeeze. Go for ten, because more than likely only eight will turn up. And if, by some freak circumstance, all ten appear? Just bunch up place settings around the table and throw a handful more pasta into the saucepan. At dinner parties, too many are better than too few; it makes for more congeniality and livelier conversation. Besides, the alternatives are yawning gaps around your table or hastily drafting in your children to fill the missing places.

Can just one half of a couple be asked on his/her own? Yes. Wives often grumble – with justification – of party invitations being withdrawn once it's discovered that their husbands won't be able to come along too. Every couple is made up of two individuals, each of whom deserves to be valued in his/her own right. Not inviting one because the other's unavailable is offensive behaviour. Either somebody's worth asking or not; it's that simple.

MENU

An unexpected, but socially disastrous, consequence of the many cookery programmes now shown on television has been the advent of ambitious amateur chefs. These are hosts who perceive every dinner party as an opportunity to show off their newly acquired culinary skills. Standards of preparation and presentation have risen (some of us are old enough to remember when half a grapefruit topped with a glacé cherry was deemed an acceptable first course) but at the expense of fundamental good manners. The host is responsible for every aspect of a party's success, of which decent food is only one element. If he/she is constantly abandoning guests to return to the kitchen, then other duties are going to be neglected, conversation will flag and some people will feel overlooked. Particularly when there's no help from a professional caterer, it's much better to serve something simple and easy rather than to offer an elaborate meal that's going to require lots of attention. Before planning a dinner menu, all hosts should make this their mantra: the reason your guests have accepted an invitation is because they like you, not because they love your food. Too little emphasis on the former and too much on the latter makes for an unsuccessful party.

Still feeling adventurous? Do feel free to serve something a bit different but not so unusual that your guests constantly have to ask, 'What is it?' followed by a suspicious sniff. Nor should your explanation be so long-winded that it dominates table talk for the next ten minutes. And no reciting of recipes during the meal. 'How did you make it?' is a polite formality and not to be interpreted literally.

When planning your menu, you'll already know who's on the guest list and who suffers from what allergies (because you'll have checked this when extending the invitation), but don't forget to quiz all guests about their current diets. At least one of the people coming will be on an extremely complex carbohydrate-free or no-protein regime. You'll want to take this into account when planning your menu (although the well-behaved guest knows better than to turn into a Food Dictator).

As the Walker Brothers memorably sang, 'Make it Easy on Yourself'. Work out a menu that will be not only delicious but also not too labour-intensive. Is it really worth sweating for a week in the kitchen over food that will be consumed in an hour?

Only cook what you can and always practise beforehand. Stick with tried and tested recipes that have never been known to let you down (although, of course, there's a first time for everything ...).

Despite being sensible and playing safe, the food still somehow goes wrong? Don't bother trying to pretend otherwise. Immediately admit to your guests what's happened with an easy laugh. It's not a tragedy (in fact, claim that your cooking's always been a joke). No one died or was even injured, aside from that nasty burn on your wrist. And no one, after all, came to your home in the guise of a professional food critic. Pour everybody another drink and reach for the telephone number of an excellent local take-away. Order generous quantities of replacement food and then relax. One meal was ruined, not your life.

CATERERS

Are the solution if you can't/won't cook. Best found by word of mouth, they can make your party planning much easier. Or they can make your life hell. Whichever of these is the outcome, they're going to cost you money. Because that's a certainty, it's best to know in advance exactly what you do and don't expect from your caterers. As with so many other social scenarios, you should begin by making a list of questions. This will cover everything from pre-dinner nibbles (and who's going to serve them) to napkins (and who's going to launder them). Then sit down with the caterer and work through all your queries, leaving nothing to chance. With guests due to arrive in ten minutes, it's too late to begin bickering over which one of you was supposed to be responsible for buying the wine. Is the caterer staying for the entire night (and will you be charged more as a result)? Does he/she come alone or bring along a fleet of junior staff too (and is there room to accommodate all of them in your stream-lined galley kitchen)? Do you own all the necessary cooking utensils or will the caterer need to pack certain pieces of equipment for the event? Half an hour over a cup of coffee ought to resolve most queries – particularly when you've got a well-compiled list to hand.

If you haven't worked with a specific caterer before, request a sample tasting so you can be completely confident about what's going to be served on the night. There's no need to feel embarrassed about asking for this extra service. Competent, professional caterers are used to organizing trial runs; they understand that a dinner party's food is too important to be left to chance. You don't want to discover that the combination of tuna carpaccio and raspberry coulis isn't a success only after it's been dished up as a main course and your guests are toying with the contents of their plates. An advance tasting also allows you to decide which wines will best complement the meal.

Curb your caterer's ambitions. In common with certain other professions such as hairdressing, all chefs believe that they're artists who ought to be allowed to explore their creativity untrammelled by petty concerns such as time or expense or your wish to sit down to dinner at half-eight. Be firm: if you, the client, don't want to eat lark's tongues in filo pastry, that's your prerogative. Despite a few grumbles, your caterer will produce shepherd's pie if instructed to do so.

There are two things that can cause trouble:

- The first is when a caterer makes claims that turn out to be false; after assuring you that preparing lunch for 200 is 'no trouble', you don't want to discover the caterer has never cooked a meal for more than twenty people. The result: disaster on the day as your guests are still waiting to be fed at five in the afternoon and the kitchen has gone up in flames.

↦ Alternatively, your caterer could behave as though working for you were a form of culinary slumming and treat your wish for simple fare with contempt. It's better not to employ someone like that because the only sure outcome is dissatisfaction on both sides.

The caterer is dropping the food to your house earlier in the afternoon? Insist that it comes with clear instructions about what, if anything, you have to do.

If you've hired a caterer, the amount of work left for you ought to be minimal – literally no more than popping a couple of bowls into the oven or taking a dish out of the fridge.

Never claim personal responsibility for a catered party. As in most other instances where a lie has been told, the truth will eventually come out and you'll be discredited.

SHOPPING

An essential, and often underestimated, element of the event. Before you go shopping, make a list. This will include all the obvious items such as fresh vegetables, bread, extra virgin olive oil, etc. But there ought to be more to it than just that. Here are a few other suggestions for the list:

↦ *Fall-back food:* For those times when the planned menu goes horribly wrong or extra guests turn up and the food has to be stretched further than originally intended.

↦ *Pre-dinner nibbles:* Useful for staving off the sound of hungry stomachs, especially if you discover one or two unexpected glitches in the kitchen that look like delaying the meal. Nuts, olives, crisps; put out a mix. Not so much that your guests are sated even before they've sat down to dinner, not so little that the night's first two arrivals will hoover up the lot.

↦ *Drink:* You'll remember to buy wine, vodka, mineral water. You'll forget to stock up on tonic water and a low-calorie mixer. Also remember fresh lemon and lime; a slice of each in the same glass looks terrific. Think about serving a cocktail before dinner but only if it's easy to make and doesn't involve the implementation of a noisy blender that'll erupt and splatter you with puréed passion-fruit.

- *Flowers:* Your guests might bring some, or they might not. Avoid this conundrum by buying flowers on the morning of the party. You'll want some in the living-room and also on your dining table. The former can be bigger and more splendid than the latter; as a rule, guests don't appreciate trying to talk to one another through a jungle of foliage. Table flowers should be pretty and low-lying – even some branches of ivy tied with ribbon and trailing across the cloth can look spectacular, especially if they're lit by …

- *Candles:* With age, we all look better in a softer light. And somehow candles, like champagne, possess the ability to create an instantly festive atmosphere. Have plenty of them about the house: tall clusters in the living-room (strategically placed to avoid being knocked over or brushed against by passing elbows); low tealights in coloured glass holders scattered about the table; and a scented candle in the bathroom. Candles are an inexpensive means of transforming your house into a pleasure palace for the night, making it – and your guests – look better than would ever be the case in the harsh light of day.

ARRANGING THE TABLE

Linen tablecloths and napkins look more attractive than paper ones, so it's worth investing in these if you can afford to do so.

Traditionally knives and forks are placed in order of use, working from the outside towards the centre so that those needed to eat the first course are furthest from the plate. Napkins are placed to the left of the main setting (on side plates, if you're putting these out) and glasses to the upper right. If you're serving more than one wine, glasses are also arranged outwards in order of use, with that for water located closest to the centre.

A note on napkin rings: The purpose of these is to hold each person's napkin from one meal to the next. Unless your guests are staying for a series of meals, napkin rings, therefore, have no place on a dinner party table.

That's the tradition, but the reality for you could be quite different, especially if you're asking guests to use the same knives and forks or glasses for different food and drink. What really matters is that:

- Everything's clean.
- Everything matches (or at least, it all co-ordinates in a charming, bohemian way).
- Nothing's chipped or broken (a potential health hazard).
- Your table isn't so overloaded that there's no room for guests to move comfortably. If you've put out too many knives, forks and glasses, everyone's going to feel pinched and cramped. Forget tradition and take away half of each place setting.

Once there are more than four of you sitting around a table, even for informal occasions it's worth taking the trouble to work out a seating plan. This will help the night to run more smoothly and allow you to anticipate any potential trouble spots among your guests. Think about who'd best enjoy whose company, who might be scratchy with one another (and should, therefore, be kept apart), who can manage without any help from you and who needs to be 'minded'.

When working out your table plan, mix up the party. Try to arrange that everyone is given a familiar face on one side and somebody unfamiliar on the other. That way, the chat is likely to be livelier.

You, as host, are expected to sit at the head of the table. However, if this position is placed at furthest remove from the kitchen and you're looking after the food, forget previous expectations and put yourself wherever is most convenient. There's no merit in clambering across your guests every time you need to clear plates or serve the next course.

Place cards look handsome on the table but only if there are a sufficient number of guests to justify their presence. There are only four of you for dinner – is it really that difficult to remember who's sitting where? But with a large group, it's much easier to have cards before each place on which the guest's name has been written. You'll probably have enough to do already – opening wine or serving up the first course – without having to direct people to their seats. If it's a big event where you have more than one table, a board directing guests to their places is also helpful and will speed up the process of getting everyone seated (because you're going to have a handful of guests who, despite repeated requests to do so, prefer to stand about talking until practically forced into a chair).

Should husbands and wives be separated? Definitely yes. They can eat every other meal together for the rest of their lives; in your home, they're expected, if not to sing then at least to chat for their supper.

Uneven numbers and gender imbalances – do either of these matter? Not particularly. An equal mix of both sexes at the table is the ideal but this oughtn't to be treated as holy writ. Suppose an old friend who's been working abroad for the past three years announces he's going to be in town for one night only – and it's the night you've organized to hold a dinner party. What are you going to do: not ask your friend over because that would disrupt your gender balance? Of course not.

Likewise, if one of your guests drops out at short notice, you shouldn't worry that this will mean an unequal number at table (although all of us should make sure to have at least one pal who never minds receiving last-minute invitations).

Changing places after a course? Only if absolutely necessary, otherwise it can be disruptive. Your guests will just be settling into a good conversation when suddenly they're asked to play an adult version of musical chairs. Only propose changes to your original seating plan if you can see there's a sticky patch somewhere around the table.

Note to guests: Traditionally, taking a lead from the hostess, you were expected to talk to the person on one side of your seat during the first course and then change to talk to the person on the other side during the main course. As your hostess (or host) is now likely to be dashing to and from the kitchen, she's not going to have much time to give you direction in this matter. However, it's still good manners not to focus your attention entirely on one of your neighbours at table to the exclusion of the other. Give both an equal chance.

THE ORDER OF THE NIGHT

This is the other list that you write out carefully before your dinner party. It's a countdown to the big night, starting with the names of those you've invited and what you plan to serve them and ending with the (ideal) time each course will be served. In between is a synchronized list of what needs to be done and when. Post it in the kitchen, and cross off each task as it's accomplished. If you're a regular dinner host, buy a little blackboard and some chalk for your pre-party list. Here are the key features of your campaign plan:

- Begin with your guests' Expected Time of Arrival. Make a note of it, and then add at least fifteen minutes because nobody turns up exactly when asked. You should be ready on the dot of the ETA but you should also be prepared to sit on your own for another quarter of an hour. This allows you to sip your first drink and check over the plan of campaign one more time to see that nothing has been forgotten.

- When preparing your order of the night, do allow enough time for drinks. Guests should be given around half an hour to chat and get to know one another before being ushered to the table. Don't rush them there; it implies panic on your part and that's disconcerting for everyone else.

- Even if one of your guests still hasn't arrived, don't wait beyond a certain time to go to table. Obviously, you'll have allowed a certain amount of leeway in your calculations but only a certain amount and not two hours. It's better to begin serving dinner rather than risk spoiling the food.

MUSIC

To play or not to play? Definitely not if it means you're jumping up from the table every half-hour or so to change the CD. Not if the music's so loud or intrusive that it interferes with conversation and forces your guests to shout at one another. Not if the music deserves to be listened to with respect (and, after all, few recording artists go into the studio with the deliberate intention that their work should provide the background for sociable chatter). In fact, really the only kind of music that ought to be played at a dinner party is the kind of music that's played in supermarkets or hotel lifts – and is that the kind of music you want to offer as an accompaniment to your main course? So it's probably better to play nothing at all; the sound of a group of people enjoying one another's company is the sweetest sound of all.

DRINK

Serve the same wine throughout each course, or through the entire evening. This is preferable to opening lots of different bottles. Make sure you have enough wine in the house by estimating a bottle per two people and then add one further to the total. After pouring out the first glass for your guests, you're allowed to put the bottle on the table and to encourage those present to help themselves and each other.

CLEARING AWAY
Do so speedily and on your own, because otherwise lots of conversations around the table are likely to be disrupted. If there's a great deal of clearing to be done, before dinner begins ask one of your friends to help; preferably a friend who won't take this request as an offensive insult. Other guests will volunteer their services. Unless you want your party to transfer itself to the kitchen, firmly discourage these offers. Tell your guests clearly and decisively that they're to remain in their seats unless/until asked to do otherwise. You're the host, you're in charge.

UNEXPECTED EXTRAS
What to do when guests arrive with two uninvited (and possibly unknown) people? Well, clearly they have committed a grave solecism by bringing extras without first asking your permission. But kicking up a stink won't make things any better. Nor will it do much for your reputation as a gracious host. For the moment, smile through gritted teeth, welcome all the new arrivals and hand them a drink before dashing to the kitchen to peel a few more potatoes.

SMOKERS AT TABLE
Sorry nicotine addicts, it's no longer acceptable. The risks of passive smoking are too high and too well known for you to light up in the company of other people. A thoughtful host, recognizing your weakness, will have set aside a space, either inside or out, where smoking's allowed. That's your territory. The dinner table isn't.

Thursday Night Kitchen Suppers, Weekend Lunches and All Other Casual Get-Togethers

An informal gathering provides the ideal opportunity to invite people you've met recently and don't know well. Just warn them in advance that this is a casual occasion and make your menu as simple as possible. Think old-fashioned food that's now rarely served and will, therefore, be enormously popular. Dishes like Irish stew are easy to make but taste wonderful. They also have the advantage of being one-pot wonders, so all you need to add for the main course is a fresh green salad.

Because the meal's casual, delegate as much as you like except when it comes to drink. Here you need to remain in control. As before, make sure you've stocked up well on adequate supplies of both the alcoholic and non-alcoholic varieties and that there's enough to last the entire party. Kick off your casual kitchen supper with a cocktail. For weekend lunch parties, have a jug of Bloody Mary prepared (and a Virgin Mary for the teetotallers).

Dance Music for Parties

Is an essential component of the successful big party. Make sure that you're well organized in advance.

Set aside one room specifically for dancing. Not all your guests will want to dance all the time; some of them will have learnt/been advised never to do so and some of them will prefer to talk to one another. A designated dance room is best.

Can you afford a DJ? Has one of your friends always yearned for a career in music? By the time the dancing begins, you're going to be too busy/tired to take responsibility for spinning the discs. This is another task that's best delegated. Also, if one person's clearly in charge, it stops all the other guests pitching in and coming to blows over whether The Clash or The Weather Girls should be played first.

Prepare the music in advance. This will stop people wreaking havoc with your CD collection. Any discs that you definitely don't want played ought to be locked away before the party.

Choose music that everyone can dance to, not some obscure indie band that you admire and that will clear the designated dance room in a matter of seconds. None of them may be to your taste, but here are half a dozen disco-era records that ALWAYS get people grooving along:

- Earth, Wind & Fire: 'Boogie Wonderland'
- Gloria Gaynor: 'I Will Survive'
- Heatwave: 'Boogie Nights'
- KC and the Sunshine Band: 'That's the Way (I Like It)'
- The Jacksons: 'Blame it on the Boogie'
- The Nolans: 'I'm in the Mood for Dancing'

Also include some slow tracks in the mix. A number of your guests will be keen to demonstrate the depth of their love for one another.

Work-Related Entertaining

Work-related entertaining ought to be no different from any other kind. However, it's possible that, because your professional life's involved, you'll be more apprehensive than usual.

There's really no need to worry. Whether you secure that big contract or not isn't dependent on the quality of your consommé. Never regard this as an opportunity to show off/ over-extend yourself/be too flash. Stay strictly within your means and your abilities, and everything should be fine. Offer precisely the same hospitality that you would to friends, serve the same food and drink, behave in the same way. In other words, be yourself. However, if you're very anxious about the state of your home or of your cooking skills, take any work-related guests to a restaurant.

3. Staying Over

Weekends away and holiday visits provide a wonderful opportunity to bond with friends. However, as on any other occasion when a group of supposed adults are placed in close proximity to one another, friction is always possible. There are certain steps both guests and hosts can take to avoid bad feeling.

A Weekend with Friends

ADVICE TO GUESTS

The weekend begins on Friday evening and ends after lunch on Sunday, but it's best to check in advance what time your hosts would like you to arrive and leave. During the same call ask if any activities have been organized for the weekend and whether particular clothes will be needed.

Accept in advance that as far as possible you must fit in with your hosts' plans. It might be your custom to stay in bed late on Sunday morning, but if they expect everyone in the house to go to church then you're not entitled to be the exception.

SHOULD GUESTS HELP?

There's nothing more luxurious than visiting a house where staff are available to attend to the needs of hosts and their guests, including you. But, sadly, that rarely happens today. Much more often, the same people who've asked us to their homes will also be responsible for cooking meals, washing dishes and performing all the other menial tasks involved in entertaining visitors. Good staff now are as rare as good guests – and much more expensive too.

It's important that you help wherever, whenever and however possible. Aside from offering your services in the kitchen this could be through volunteering to assist with certain practical matters like clearing the table or even setting it before dinner if your hosts appear particularly harried. Do be careful, though, not to force your help on people who don't want it. They may prefer you wouldn't carry a pile of dirty plates into the kitchen, for example, because then you'll discover their behind-the-scenes slovenly habits. And if everyone leaps up from the table to help clear dishes, the merry conversation your hosts have been carefully nurturing will probably die away. It's easy to cause harm in the belief that you're doing good, so offer practical assistance with the understanding that it might be refused. Your hosts will still be grateful for the kind thought.

Besides, there are lots of other ways to be a helpful guest. If you know whoever's invited you will be preparing the whole meal, ask if you can bring one of the courses. Or you could enquire in advance what's being served and offer to bring along appropriate wine. Actually it's a good idea always to telephone before a visit and ask what you might bring, especially as your hosts will usually then reply, 'Just yourself,' which leaves you with the pleasant thought that you're better than any bottle of vintage champagne.

When visiting people who are clearly trying to accomplish several things simultaneously such as putting their children to bed while cooking dinner, recognize that you can be helpful by taking on one of their roles: assume responsibility for pouring everyone a drink (including a large one for the harassed host); keep the conversation going while your hosts are out of the room; chat to a guest who doesn't know anyone else present. Hosts won't always need your help but they'll be happy it was offered.

ABSENCE
Really will make your hosts' hearts grow fonder. Bear this in mind each time you're asked to stay with friends. Don't expect them to have arranged a sequence of activities to occupy and amuse you. Avoid being discovered listlessly hanging around the table at the end of breakfast wondering what to do next. Use the opportunity to catch up with your own correspondence (even if this really means going into the garden to text absent friends on your mobile phone).

Bring with you a book you've been meaning to read, a portable CD player/radio, or even some work that needs to be finished. Although be careful with the last of these; you're not

entitled to turn someone else's home into an extension of your office. If you've brought your car, make a visit to some local town or place of interest, even perhaps offer to do some shopping for the house? Above all, show that you're mature enough not to need constant minding.

A word of warning: avoid appearing too independent, otherwise you can give the erroneous impression of treating your hosts' home as little more than a free hotel. Always ask if they've made any plans for the day, explain your own intentions and confirm the exact time at which you're expected to appear for lunch or pre-dinner drinks. That way, you ought to be missed in your absence and welcomed on your return.

A note on tipping: If you're staying with people for a day or two and they employ any staff – even just someone local who comes in to clean one morning a week – it's considered good manners on your departure to leave behind a small financial remuneration. Leave a folded cash note (or several) beside your bed where it can easily be found when the room's next cleaned. There are no absolute rules about the size of this tip. It depends how long you've been staying and the amount of service you've enjoyed. Be generous but not to the point of excess, otherwise you'll just seem flashy. If you're not sure what's the best thing to do, quietly ask your hosts for guidance.

The same rule is applicable when you're staying in a rented house that comes with staff. The owners will have paid the basic salary (or you will, as part of your rental charge) but you'll find some tipping is also required. Failure to give additional money will result in sour looks from the people who've been pandering to your various whims over the previous few days. Staff remember who are good and who are bad tippers. If you're hoping to stay with the same hosts again, it's best to be included in the former category.

Naturally none of the above is relevant if you know it's your hosts who'll be changing the bed and sweeping the floor after you've gone. Leave money under those circumstances and they'll probably think you're becoming forgetful and return it to you. There are plenty of ways of thanking friends for their hospitality that don't involve the direct transfer of cash.

House Borrowing

Just because your hosts aren't present, this shouldn't make you any less of a good guest. Whatever the circumstances – friends suggest you borrow their cottage in the country for a couple of days or they're going to be out of the city during your visit but insist you stay in their apartment anyway – still behave as though they're present at all times. Do nothing your generous friends wouldn't be happy to witness. That means no inviting other people over for drinks, a meal or sex.

Conduct your social life off the premises, even if the proposed visitors are known to your absent hosts. Most of us have powerfully proprietorial instincts and don't relish the idea of anyone in our homes without advance notice. And there's an absolute ban on snooping. However tempting it might be just to peep into your hosts' bedroom or run an eye over their photograph albums, resist the urge.

Leave the place as you found it on your arrival. How awful to come back to a house you've lent and find week-old dishes still sitting unwashed in the sink. If you've broken anything, replace it or – should lack of time/opportunity prohibit you from doing this – leave an apologetic note offering to do so. Keep aside an hour before your departure to run round the place making sure it's as clean as (if not cleaner than) when you first arrived. Don't leave dirty sheets on the bed or used towels thrown about the bathroom; fold all these up neatly and leave them ready to be laundered. Some hosts leave instructions about using the washing machine and dryer; in these circumstances, good manners demand you do as requested.

Should you know your hosts will be returning almost immediately after your departure, you could buy some fresh flowers to await their arrival. What about stocking the fridge with delicious food so that they don't have to worry about preparing dinner on their first night back? A few bottles of wine? Or a gift voucher for a specialist shop in the area? Having had a chance to glance over their bookshelves and music collection, you'll be in a position to pick out a gift that reflects their tastes. Of course, you don't have to leave a present at all, but the one item that should be discovered by hosts as evidence of your recent visit is a card saying thank you. Never shut the door after borrowing someone else's house without acknowledging this act of generosity.

TIDINESS

While enjoying the hospitality of other people, you must be the very embodiment of neatness. After using a cup, don't leave it in the sink for someone else (most likely your host) to discover later. Wash, dry and put the thing back where you found it. When staying in another house, leave your bedroom so tidy that it could give the impression of being unused. Straighten cushions and stack newspapers neatly, return books to the shelves, fold the towels after using them in the bathroom. This behaviour mightn't be customary for you at home, but for the moment you must curb that desire to express your exuberant personality by leaving traces of yourself everywhere.

Alternatively, you might have a powerfully anal-retentive character, washing your hands every half-hour, trailing a finger across window sills to check for dust, scanning all knives and forks for any residue of grease, that kind of thing. And then you find yourself spending time with those enchanting hosts, Mr and Mrs Slob. They, and their many rumbustious children, don't seem to be overly preoccupied by the need to wash – either themselves or anything they own.

Entering the Slob household, you're gripped with terror at the idea of touching a chair, a plate, the food on it. Salmonella, or worse, seems the probable if not certain legacy of your visit. Under these circumstances, despite a powerful urge to do so, you may not slip on a pair of latex gloves, begin boiling kettles and apply quantities of disinfectant to anything within reach. You can, politely, refuse a drink or a meal. You cannot, however, start hoovering the carpet or dusting the pictures. You can straighten the cushions and covers of the armchair you're about to sit in. Your visit will undoubtedly be brief and never repeated. It's probably best to go straight home and calm your frazzled nerves by rearranging the sock drawer.

Advice to Hosts

ARE YOU READY FOR GUESTS?

Inviting guests to stay in your home is quite different from asking them over for a meal. It involves a great deal more intimacy than is often experienced between two friends. You're nervous about having people to stay? The thought of staying with you is liable to leave them feeling every bit as nervous. Before extending an invitation, you ought to ask yourself the following questions:

- Will I mind finding someone else's hair in the shower?
- Will I mind being seen in my threadbare but deeply comfortable dressing-gown?
- Will I mind discovering an unwashed cup in the sink, smears of jam all over the butter and an empty milk carton in the fridge?

❧ Will I mind that my proposal to 'treat the place as though it's your own home' has been taken quite so literally?

Provided the answer to all the above questions is a decisive no, you're ready to become an overnight host. Definitely don't ask people to stay if you're going to be furious when the bathroom door's locked and you hear cheery singing from the other side as all the hot water fills a guest's bath. Or if you hate talking to anyone first thing in the morning. Or if the sight of a book out of place leaves you grinding your teeth.

PREPARING THE HOUSE FOR GUESTS

Your usual habit of wandering around the house wearing nothing other than a shrunken T-shirt will have to be temporarily abandoned. Likewise your fondness for eating cold baked beans directly from the tin or your tendency to watch television at three in the morning when hit by insomnia. Within the privacy of our own homes, all of us are free to indulge in various personal eccentricities. But once people come to stay, you lose both that freedom and that privacy. Obviously it's still your home but that doesn't mean you can do whatever you like without a moment's thought for anybody else. A good host will always put the guest's needs first.

Hide everything private out of sight, whether letters from an old boyfriend or your extensive collection of bondage equipment. If you leave evidence of your personal life lying around, it will be seen, and noted, and commented on later – although not to you. Instead, people you've never met will come to hear about those fur-trimmed handcuffs.

Clean the house. That point ought to be obvious, but, as plenty of guests can testify, not all hosts have grasped it.

Make the place welcoming. You might prefer to live with the curtains permanently closed, but your guests should be given the option of a little daylight. Open windows to let fresh air circulate and put some flowers in the living-room.

Examine your home for possible traps. You've been meaning to get the kitchen's electrical socket fixed for the past five years but have never got around to doing so. Put a warning notice beside it, otherwise the hapless guest who'd planned to make some toast could end up being toasted. Loose cables snaking across the spare-bedroom floor, locks that need to be turned three times in an anti-clockwise direction if you're ever to escape from the downstairs toilet, an unexpected little step leading from the kitchen to the back door. You're used to these hazards; your house guest will be encountering them for the first time. Try to make the encounter as pleasant and unlethal as possible. Otherwise the visit could end with a trip to the nearest Accident and Emergency Department followed by a hefty compensation demand.

THE GUEST BEDROOM
This should contain the following essentials:

- *A decent, comfortable bed:* One with a firm base and good mattress (NB like the room, this must be spotlessly clean).
- *Adequate bedlinen:* 'Adequate' does not mean shiny pink nylon that emits electric shocks whenever it's touched. The bedlinen will, naturally, be clean and well ironed (*Tip:* Iron with spray starch which, together with tissue paper, is one of the most undervalued inventions of the past century). Ideally the bedlinen will also be matching or at least of the same colour. On the other hand, antique sheets and pillowcases mixed together can look charming. Duvet or sheets and blankets? That's your call.
- *Plenty of pillows:* So you sleep with your head resting on a thin plank of wood? Not everyone will want to share this ascetic pleasure. Some people like a hard pillow, others prefer something soft. Put a mixture of both on the bed. It's always

better to provide too many rather than too few pillows; the surplus can be left to one side. And besides, your guest will be so entertained by the mixture of books and magazines left on the bedside table (see below) that lots of pillows will be needed for support during late-night reading.

- *A bedside lamp* to stand on the small table next to the bed. A bedside lamp means your visitor, cosily settled, doesn't have to throw back the covers to switch off the central light and then fumble a return across the room in darkness. Or wake up in the middle of the night and stub a toe on the way to the toilet. By the way, don't forget to check that the bulb works.
- *Clean towels,* and plenty of them. Stacked according to size, there ought to be a face cloth, hand towel and bath towel. Add an extra one to this mix; it mightn't be used but you never know.
- *A spare blanket or two:* Leave these somewhere convenient, not necessarily on the bed but not in a cupboard either (unless, of course, you relish the idea of guests rooting through your drawers in search of extra bedding). Just as some of us sleep with the central heating turned up to maximum and others insist on open windows even in the middle of winter, so different people prefer different quantities of cover in bed.
- *Fresh water and a glass:* In case your guest becomes thirsty in the middle of the night or has to take some medication before sleep.

You might also like to include the following thoughtful extras:

- *Books and magazines:* Choose these with your guest in mind. The guest bedroom makes a natural home for back issues of general-interest magazines, anything from *The Economist* to

Vanity Fair. Even months after their publication, they still contain features that can be read.

Books left in the guest bedroom should reflect the interests/tastes of your guest. This is also a good place to leave publications about the local area.

- A *small flask of whiskey* (for the proverbial nightcap) and a tin of biscuits. Owing to your generous hospitality elsewhere in the house, neither of these is likely to be touched, but you never know …
- *An alarm clock:* One that's easy to use and doesn't require a degree in engineering.
- A small but welcoming *bowl of flowers.*
- A rack holding some *postcards* so that your guests can write to friends saying what a nice time they're having during their stay with you.
- *A radio and/or a television:* Just warn guests not to play this at top volume while you're trying to sleep on the other side of a thin partition wall.

Although the above advice might suggest that having overnight guests involves a lot of time and effort, this really isn't the case. Chocolate on the pillow and lavatory paper left pointed into a triangle – what are you, the latest outpost of an American hotel chain? Relax. These are your friends coming to stay, not the editors of *Condé Nast Traveller.*

You haven't got a spare bedroom but you are expecting a house guest? Not to worry, all that's needed is a daybed or convertible sofabed in the living-room. In these circumstances, if you're going to entertain visitors regularly, it might be worth buying a low screen that can be pushed around the bed at night, just to give your guest a little extra privacy. And don't forget all the other essentials such as a good lamp, bottle of water, bowl of flowers, etc.

THE GUEST BATHROOM

Whether you have one for your visitor's exclusive use or whether you'll be sharing the same space, give some thought to the following:

- The room should be clean. It should remain clean. This means you'll have to check on its condition regularly while guests are staying with you.
- Keep a supply of extra towels to hand. Yes, you've already left an ample number in the guest bedroom, but your visitor might have forgotten to bring one into the bathroom. Without any spares available, the only alternative will be to use your towel – is that what you want?
- Bathmats – lots of them. It's amazing how much water some people manage to splash about the place. A bathmat will help to soak up most of this.
- Decent lights that actually work, especially over the sink.
- A scented candle and something to light it. *Tip:* To help clear unpleasant odours in a bathroom, leave a box of matches by the toilet. Lighting one burns up the noxious fumes in the atmosphere and is infinitely preferable to the nauseating scent of so-called air fresheners.
- Bathroom treats and necessities such as shower gel and bath oil, shampoo and hair conditioner. This is an excellent time to put out the items you purloined from a hotel bathroom in Marbella; your guests won't feel guilty using them.
- Some hosts like to provide extras such as a toothbrush and toothpaste, nail files, shoe cleaning kit, etc. These are thoughtful bonuses but it's safe to say that most guests today travel with their own toothbrush (unless they're unable to drive home after a party).
- Leave an explanatory note in the bathroom if anything doesn't work properly – i.e. 'Flush loo twice please.'

◆ Drawn like the proverbial moths to a flame, guests will look in bathroom cupboards, so if you don't want them to discover your preference for fruit-flavoured condoms, don't leave any there.

WHEN GUESTS ARRIVE

Lay down any house rules – but nicely.

If there's only enough hot water in the morning for showers, not baths, make this clear at once (and not through gritted teeth the following day after you've had to endure a cold shower).

You're planning to sit down to dinner at eight o'clock? Let your guests know now, rather than presume they'll guess and then feeling cross when they turn up at half past eight.

This is also the moment to tell them about anywhere that's out-of-bounds or unsafe, show them how the rug in the hall rucks up at one end and trips the unwary or how the dishwasher can unexpectedly bolt across the kitchen floor. And show guests where they can find anything that might be needed during their stay, otherwise you're likely to come across them frantically opening doors in an effort to find the toilet.

While you're happy to make your overnight guests' stay a pleasure, if they're leaving early in the morning, are you obliged to be out of bed, washed, groomed and ready to cook a full breakfast? Not necessarily. You're a private host rather than a professional hotelier and that deserves to be taken into account. All guests have a duty to be considerate – and self-sufficient too. Show any early departures where to find whatever will be required before they head off, set the table for breakfast, leave a note saying how much you've enjoyed having them to stay (and reminding them to close the front door firmly but quietly on their way out) and leave it at that. At six o'clock in the morning. you're under no obligation to wave them a fond goodbye.

Holiday Guests

You're likely to behave quite differently while on holiday from the way you would in your familiar environment. Think carefully, therefore, about inviting anyone else to join you as a guest while you're away from home. This could be the only fortnight in the year that you don't have to go to work every day. The intention is that you relax completely and don't worry about mundane tasks like shopping and cleaning. But then you ask some good friends to come along too. Their presence can quickly become an irritant, especially if they give the constant impression of needing to be fed and entertained. Instead of being able to unwind by the pool, you find yourself involved in a round of ferrying other people to and from airports and railway stations, worrying about what to cook for (yet another) big dinner and organizing excursions to local places of interest. You then return from the holiday feeling completely exhausted and hostile towards your hapless guests, none of whom has any idea that they've inspired a rage of resentment in their host. Bear this in mind, therefore, before issuing an invitation, no matter how good an idea it might seem. Otherwise you could lose both a holiday and a friend.

ADVICE TO HOSTS
If you have extended the offer, what's the best way to make sure your guests' visit runs smoothly? State from the beginning if expenses are to be shared or if you'll be carrying the bulk of all household costs. You don't want to be shy about this, because it's going to cost you money. There's no need to curse yet another large supermarket bill while your visitors sprawl on sun loungers downing a few more bottles of the local wine. Of course, the best guests offer to pay their own way (or at least

make a point of buying a couple of cases of that local wine) but sometimes a little prompting on your part will be needed.

Encourage your visitors to show self-sufficiency and independence. On holiday, they ought to rely on you, their host, for as little as possible. Play down your own role so that you're all equally responsible for the daily running of the house. Make sure everyone undertakes an equal share of shopping for household provisions, of preparing meals, of keeping the place in order.

Back to that point about hosts sometimes behaving differently when removed from their usual surroundings. You could discover that you don't actually like the people you've invited to join you on holiday – or indeed they could take an irrational dislike to you when asked to stir off the sunlounger and help with preparations for lunch. Although they're supposed to be relaxing, shared holidays can actually be terribly stressful. Like Christmas, they come with such a weight of expectations that disappointment seems almost inevitable. You have been warned: issue invitations with care.

4. Formal Social Occasions

The most important fact about an invitation card is that it conveys the necessary news that you're giving a party and you want the recipient to come along. So, when preparing an invitation, operate on the who/when/where/what/how principle.

Invitations

You need to include all the key pieces of information succinctly in the following fashion:

- Who are you, the party giver?
- When is the party?
- Where is it taking place?
- What sort of party is it?
- How are guests to dress?

Cover these five points, and nothing's left to chance.

Ideally, this information should be typed/printed/photo-copied and standardized for all guests. Then, in handwriting, you add anything extra – such as the invitee's name or a request to come early/stay late.

To run through the five points in a little more detail:

- Who are you? Give your name in full, especially if you're not necessarily best friends with some of your guests (who'll not know that your nickname's Fluffy and, therefore, stare in baffled stupefaction when an invitation arrives from this source).
- When's the party? That means giving the date (including the year) and also the time. If it's a drinks-followed-by-dinner occasion, state the time of both. Grand invitations often include an estimated time of guests' departure (usually courtesy of some old-fashioned euphemism such as 'Carriages at 1 a.m.'). If you're giving a drinks party, it's not only permissible to announce when this event will begin and end, it's advisable (six to eight is the norm).
- Where's the party? In the same way that it's helpful to give your full name, so there are advantages to providing a full address, again in case not everyone has visited the place before, or can remember how to get there. Worried that some of your guests won't find their way? Include a map with your invitation – and also a telephone number they can call if lost or late.
- Make it clear what sort of party you're asking guests to attend. Yes, it's a wedding, but what sort of ceremony? Outdoors, in what was until two days earlier, a cow-field? Every woman who turns up in kitten-heel slingbacks is going to curse you for not warning her in advance to throw a pair of old boots into the back of the car. Will there be any food, or should everyone eat beforehand? Are you providing a free bar or expecting guests to pay for their drinks after the first couple of rounds? You don't have to write a pre-party treatise; you do have to give some guidance.
- And that includes the question of clothes. If you don't notify guests of the occasion's dress code, then like Cole Porter's song, it'll be a case of 'Anything Goes'. One man will be in a

suit, the other in jeans; one woman will be wearing her new evening dress, the other her favourite T-shirt. Remember, it's your party, you're entitled to specify a dress code; the majority of your guests will appreciate being notified in advance what they should wear.

THE FORMAL INVITATION

This is now most often despatched for a wedding:

> *Mr and Mrs Patrick Plodd*
> *request the pleasure of your company*
> *at the marriage of their daughter*
> *Patricia*
>
> *to*
>
> *Mr Anthony Ashwood*
> *at St Bridget's Church, Ballybraiden*
> *on Friday, 13th May at two o'clock*
> *and afterwards at The Ballybraiden Arms Hotel*

Evening Dress   *RSVP*
                                   The Moorings
                                   Ballybraiden

THE INFORMAL INVITATION

> *Patricia and Tony*
> *are delighted to invite you*
> *to their wedding*
> *at St Bridget's Church, Ballybraiden*
> *at 2 p.m. on Friday, 13th May*
> *and then for drinks, dinner and dancing at*
> *The Ballybraiden Arms Hotel*
>
> *Evening Dress*
>
> *Please let us know before Friday, 30th April*
> *if you can come along by emailing Patricia on:*
> *Pat.Tony@hotmail.com*

Much the same invitation as the first, although this time it's being sent out directly in the names of the bride and groom rather than that of the bride's parents, and the style is a bit more casual.

Whatever form of invitation you choose to send, it'll look smarter if the card and envelope match, so try to make sure this is always the case. It doesn't actually matter what format you use for your invitations, whether incredibly formal or the last word in casual. What matters is that the necessary information is conveyed to guests in as concise a manner as possible. After that, it's simply a question of personal preference. There's no reason why you should feel obliged to follow tradition or precedent if this doesn't reflect your own style and outlook.

For major events, such as a wedding, the invitation proper ought to be posted off to prospective guests between six weeks and two months in advance of the date. However, wise planners will often provide even earlier, more informal warning, maybe through a phone call or email that asks their friends to keep a particular day free. By doing this, you can be confident that the people you really want at your party will be present.

Posting out printed invitations indicates that you're giving quite a serious party. It also implies that you'd like to know beforehand who will and won't be coming. There are a number of ways to encourage recipients to inform you of their intentions. One is to have the letters RSVP (*répondez s'il vous plaît*) printed at the bottom right-hand corner of your card. Below this, give an address, telephone number and perhaps even email address to which replies can be sent. You might also opt to provide a deadline for replies. While this can look a little too bossy, it certainly helps when finalizing the catering arrangements.

Organizers of major events like weddings usually now include another card with the invitation; this is a prepared reply form that confirms whether the person invited can or cannot attend. The card will come with a pre-addressed envelope. If you're sending them out, providing a stamp is a nice touch and will make the process of responding to your invitation even easier for guests.

Nevertheless, there are some people out there in partyland who seem congenitally incapable of replying to invitations. You might have to make a few phone calls ahead of the event to check whether these individuals plan to be present or not. They're your friends; it's up to you to suffer their foibles. Don't like to make the calls yourself? Ask a family member or someone else to do it for you.

GUESTS WHO RECEIVE AN INVITATION
The form it takes will give you a good indication of how you ought to respond. Asked by card, reply by card; asked by phone, reply by phone; sent an email, send similar back.

But whatever method you use to reply, be speedy. Any host will be able to tell you about the irritation of waiting for a guest to confirm attendance at a big party. Should someone else be asked instead? Does the table plan need to be revised? Will special dietary requirements demand consideration when planning the lunch menu?

Business-related events tend to come with a request to reply before a certain date; invitations to private parties are less likely to carry the same demand. But good manners dictate that you let your hosts know as soon as possible whether you'll be turning up or not.

Is the invitation unclear about the specific nature of the party? This happens all the time: an invitation card arrives asking you to come to a friend's house in a fortnight's time but whether you're going to be offered a drink or full dinner seems vague. The best solution is to telephone and ask for clarification.

Unsure if you're going to be free? Telephone the people

who've sent you an invitation and explain your predicament –
provided this isn't an instance when you're holding out for a
better offer from someone/somewhere else (in which case,
shame on you). Ask the hosts whether there's some kind of
unofficial deadline for acceptance or refusal and commit yourself to giving an answer before that date. In cases of uncertainty,
suggest that it might be simpler if you were 'disinvited'. Ideally,
the party-giver will immediately insist you do no such thing and
declare that your company will be very much wanted, even up
to the last moment. But brace yourself for acceptance of the idea.

Can you bring someone else with you to a party? Only if that
person's name is on the invitation or a non-specific extra is
invited, such as 'and partner'. In any case, it's important when
replying to clarify whether you'll be coming to the party alone
or with someone else – and ideally, give the name of the someone so that it'll be known to your hosts in advance (useful if
they want to write place cards for the table).

Don't imagine yourself entitled to ring up and ask can you
bring your girlfriend or, even worse, just turn up with her. It's
not your party, you're not in charge of the guest list. You'll either
have to face temporary separation from the girlfriend or not go
to the event.

The same rule applies to children. If they're not mentioned
on the invitation, leave the darlings at home with a baby-sitter
and be grateful for the opportunity to have a few hours away
from them.

What if you're one half of a couple, both of you have been
asked but one of you can't make the party? Contact your hosts
and explain this scenario before asking if you can bring someone else instead (never presume this is allowed). Once you've
received permission – as you ought – say who'll be coming with
you and, if this person's not known to the hosts, provide a little
background information.

Weddings

An entire industry has developed around the wedding ceremony, creating self-described 'specialists' in everything from cakes to hairdressing for the big day. So we'll leave most of that advice to the experts and confine ourselves to a few pertinent points.

The first of these relates to common sense. Yes, it's an important day, but it's only one out of your entire life. And frankly, the more emphasis you place on the day, the less likely you are to enjoy it. Does the precise consistency of the first course salad dressing really matter that much? In years to come, will your guests remember what shade of pink the bridesmaid's floral bouquets were? Can a single misprint in the Order of Service booklet really justify your bursting into tears and declaring that the whole day's been ruined?

Try to keep everything in perspective and remember what matters most is that you and your guests participate in an enjoyable and memorable occasion. Nothing else is of as much consequence.

In the months and weeks leading up to the wedding, avoid all arguments. So your future mother-in-law wants to wear puce? Let her. So the make-up artist booked last year is suddenly not available? Hire another one. The bride insists on walking up the aisle without shoes through rose petals? That's her choice (but make sure she's prepared to foot the bill – so to speak – for all those denuded roses). The best man won't hire a morning suit? So be it.

Stay calm and stay focused. This occasion is about two people publicly attesting their love for one another and expressing the desire to remain together for the rest of their lives. Whether they do so in Druidic costume on a mountainside or in a cathedral attended by full orchestra and choir, the sentiment remains the same.

Now a couple of practical points. Before your wedding, clearly work out the kind of event that you want to hold and the amount of money that you're prepared to spend. Try to match the first with the second but expect some compromising to be necessary. Once this is done, don't waiver, no matter what the temptation. Decisiveness will make your preparations easier and less fraught.

Draw up an action plan and a timetable chart on which all preparatory organization is shown chronologically, starting with today and counting down to the wedding day itself. This simple device greatly narrows the chances of something being forgotten, whether it was icing the cake or buying a thank-you present for the Matron of Honour.

If you can afford to do so, hire a wedding planner – the best your money can buy. Hand over all responsibility to this person and assume that he/she is competent to do the job. If you can't afford a wedding planner, then delegate, delegate, delegate. But having done so, let go. Don't delegate and then interfere. If your Aunt Gloria has been given responsibility for the catering, leave it to her. Your father said he'd have the car washed and bedecked with white ribbon before the two of you set off for church? Take him at his word.

Whatever approach you're taking to your wedding, please keep it to yourself until the day. Brides are like first-time parents or first-time home owners: they imagine no one else has ever done this before and that their experiences are of universal interest. They're not and you risk sorely trying your friends' patience by talking on, and on, and on about the wedding.

One final observation. In the week before the wedding, someone will throw a tantrum or a knife or possibly both. Just don't let it be you, but be ready to mop up tears or blood. Regardless of how well prepared you are, nerves will get strained to breaking point.

A note on stag and hen parties: These aren't, as a rule, renowned for being occasions when everyone behaves impeccably. In fact, the well-mannered stag party would probably be regarded as a catastrophic failure. But that doesn't mean the only alternative is behaving badly. All you need to do is spare a moment's thought for other people's feelings. Everyone in the group walking through the city centre wearing giant plastic penises? Hilarious, except for parents who have to explain the phenomenon to their young children. Everyone in the group staying in the restaurant until four o'clock in the morning? Great fun, except for the staff who have to stay behind after you to clear up. Everyone in the group then so drunk that a spontaneous song marathon breaks out on the street? Memorable, particularly for local residents who are woken up by the racket.

It's the groom or bride's last weekend of freedom – but they're not released from the responsibility of showing a little consideration. And that applies to the rest of you as well.

WEDDING CEREMONY

No need to dwell here on the style of the wedding – again, there are more than enough other sources of advice on this subject. Instead, a few helpful pointers for both the principals and secondary characters.

BRIDE AND GROOM

While it's unquestionably your day, you're not the only two people present. So, in the midst of your personal happiness, spare a thought for everyone else. Hold the ceremony on the top of a mountain and it's unlikely that your wheelchair-bound grandmother will make it – unless she's going to be lowered into position by helicopter.

A sister has just broken up with her long-time boyfriend who's also coming to the wedding? Keep them well apart at table.

One of the bridesmaid's a vegetarian? Let the caterers know so a separate menu can be arranged for her.

In other words, don't become so wrapped up in yourselves that you forget there's still a whole other world out there; several hundred of its representatives are planning to get dressed up and watch you both make your vows.

BRIDESMAIDS
At least one of you will hate the dress you've been given to wear. But:

- It has cost you nothing.
- You only have to wear the thing for one day.
- The bride's your oldest friend – looking like a mauve helium balloon is the least you could do for her.

One of you will be single and without any prospects of getting married. You will, therefore, become sentimentally maudlin at some point during the speeches. The other bridesmaids should recognize that this is going to happen and be prepared – with clean tissues and supportive words.

One of you (possibly, but not necessarily, the bridesmaid who's congenitally single) will drink too much and need to be assisted to a quiet room where you'll be extremely sick before falling asleep. The following day, you'll have to apologize for your behaviour to the bride and groom, blaming the crash diet followed for the past fortnight in order to fit into a dress that you hated wearing anyway.

One of you will make a fool of yourself with one of the groomsmen.

As thanks for your services, the groom will give you all an expensive trinket. None of you will like, or ever wear, this. You will, however, sound appropriately grateful for the gift.

BEST MAN

You have three official duties – and therefore three opportunities either to make yourself useful or make a mistake.

- You stand beside the groom before the ceremony begins while he waits for the bride's arrival. As he's probably hungover from the night before (and you could be in a similar condition because you were in the pub together until closing time) bring along something in the way of a 'cure'.
- At the appropriate moment during the ceremony, you produce the wedding ring from your pocket. This is not at all similar to producing a white rabbit from a top hat, but it's amazing how many best men find the task beyond their abilities. Put the ring into your jacket pocket the night before the wedding – and before you and the groom go to the pub. That way, it'll already be in place when needed.
- You make a speech at the meal/party held after the wedding ceremony. The primary purpose of this speech is to give some insight into the groom's history and character. It is not an ideal opportunity to discuss his addiction to lap-dancing clubs or the brevity of his two previous marriages. You're here to praise the man, not bury him in opprobrium. It helps if you can be funny. It doesn't help if you're smutty. It's certainly best if you're brief. It's definitely worst if you're still talking after twenty minutes. (See *speeches* below.)

You've also one duty that is unofficial but advisable: be especially attentive to whichever bridesmaid's single and without any prospects of getting married. The bride will appreciate this consideration and not mind so much when, after the honeymoon, her new husband continues to spend as much time as ever playing pool with you in the pub.

GROOMSMEN

Are expected to direct guests to their seats before the wedding ceremony and escort the innumerable bridesmaids out of the church afterwards. Plus, they stand in the back row of group photographs smiling manically. Later, they huddle together at the bar, passing lascivious remarks about women before one of them is discovered in the car park with a bridesmaid (never the girl who's single and without any prospects of getting married).

PARENTS OF THE COUPLE

Have two functions, both of which will cause them a great deal of pain and anguish. They must:

- Pay for the wedding, together with its innumerable, and unbelievably expensive, adjuncts.
- Be polite to each other.

They will complain a lot about both but should refrain from doing so in the presence of either the bride or groom.

The groom's parents have less to do than those of the bride. The groom's father can suggest he pay for some of the costs of the day, and then grumble that he never expected to be taken up on the offer, particularly if presented with the drinks bill. The groom's mother is expected to find out what the bride's mother is wearing, and then buy something more ostentatious for herself.

The bride's father traditionally bears responsibility for paying for his daughter's wedding; he will remind her of this fact when, five years later, she tells him of plans to divorce her husband. He also escorts his daughter to the ceremony and makes a speech after it. During the first of these, he'll harangue the bride for being late as usual and during the second he'll declare that never a cross word has passed between himself and his little girl.

The bride's mother has only one task: to cry during the wedding ceremony. Then, while dabbing her eyes to check that no mascara has become smudged, she is permitted to cast covert glances at the groom's mother and speculate how any woman that age dares to wear such a short skirt.

WEDDING GUESTS
A few obvious, but essential, pieces of advice:

- Don't flirt with either the bride or the groom (at least, not too openly).
- Don't attend the event if you've been having an affair with either, or, as the Hollywood actress Tallulah Bankhead once famously commented in the middle of the marriage ceremony, with both of them.
- Don't become so carried away with the romance of the moment that you propose to someone else – particularly if you're already married.
- Don't become so drunk that you heckle the best man through his speech, goose the groom's mother, fight with aforementioned's husband and then pass out in the shrubbery after making out with someone half your age.

If any of the above seem possible, send a well-phrased note of regret accompanied by a decent wedding present and stay at home instead.

Inside a church or any other religious building, show respect for the faith it serves. That means no loud chatting or clapping, no flitting about the pews as though this were a drinks party in an unusual venue, no moving the flower arrangements to get a better angle of the bride and groom with your video camera, and no blinding whoever's conducting the ceremony with a camera flash at key moments of the ceremony. You mightn't have any religious beliefs; that's no reason to disregard the possibility that other people do. If you've brought small children with you, don't be surprised if they quickly become bored – what else did you expect when the ceremony lasts two hours? Prepare for this possibility. Bring along a book or some toys, seat yourself at the end of a row and close to the exit so that you and the children are able to leave if they become too restless. Talk to them in advance and explain what's going to happen. That way, you're less likely to encounter disapproving looks from the other guests.

Confetti looks lovely at the time, is hell to clean up later. So yes, by all means, do chuck it about – provided you're willing to come back the following morning and get rid of the soggy mess left all over the tarmac.

Otherwise, go along and have a wonderful time. Arrive before the bride walks up the aisle, leave before the caterers have finished stacking up the hired tables. Sing gustily in church, do not sing at all during the reception, even – or especially – if there's a karaoke machine on the premises. Speak to the people seated on either side of you at dinner, suppress any urge to speak to the entire room by seizing the microphone during the toasts.

Above all, enjoy yourself. Does this seem obvious? Then why is it that every wedding attracts its share of guests who perform their best bad-fairy impression? They'll be forever commemorated on video bickering with their partners, sitting on their hands while everyone else is raising a glass to the bride and groom, staring gloomily at the dancefloor (where their partners are now energetically jiving with another guest) and darkly muttering about being always the bridesmaid, never the bride. This is one occasion where you're not the main player but have been assigned a minor role in the drama – carry it out with dignity and evident pleasure.

WEDDING PRESENTS

It's a good idea to tell friends and guests what you'd like to receive, otherwise you're going to end up with a lot of casserole dishes.

For this reason, a wedding list – an assortment of suitable presents that can be bought from one or more shops – is extremely helpful. If you've put together a wedding list, inform all guests of this fact when sending them their invitations. Include a note that gives details of the shop(s). Ideally, the ordering of the present can be done by phone or over the internet. Once everything's ordered, the retailer organizes for the lot to be delivered to the newly married couple.

When drawing up a wedding list, take different budgets into account. Not all your guests are able to afford an American-style fridge-freezer for themselves, let alone for you. Have a few inexpensive items – sets of kitchen knives, table mats or napkins – on the list. They won't be ordered (who wants to look like a total cheapskate?) but their presence will show your thoughtful consideration.

Be realistic. Don't expect to receive everything on the list. When you get back from your honeymoon that set of dining chairs mightn't be waiting for you at home. Some guests prefer not to rely on wedding lists but to use their own imagination. This means you'll be given a raffia-work breadbasket instead. You're obliged to appear as grateful as you would were it the Italian chrome wine cooler on which you'd really set your heart.

Keep a note of who's given you what (the shop responsible for your wedding list can provide you with this information) and mention the gift specifically when writing to say thanks; a task, by the way, which should be accomplished within days of returning from your honeymoon. Sometimes, finding the right words to say thank you will be a challenge to your creative powers – as when making the claim that a raffia-work breadbasket was what you'd always wanted – but it'll also be good manners.

If you're both over a certain age, comfortably living together for the past five years and affluent enough to have bought your own casserole dishes, do you really need to receive wedding presents at all? How about proposing that your guests donate to a charity instead? Accompanying the invitation, send a note to this effect, preferably stating the name of the charity you'd like to help and giving full details of how a donation can be made.

Guests should note that even if you can't make the wedding, you should send a present. The purpose of the present is to show that you wish the couple well in their future together; it's not a way of repaying some of what they (or their parents) will have spent on the day.

If no wedding list is provided, ask the couple what they'd like or need. They'll then be able to let you know that they already own more than enough casserole dishes.

Don't bring your wedding present to the wedding; someone will have to take responsibility for its welfare and to make sure it doesn't go home with one of the waiters.

SPEECHES
Should be made as rarely as possible. Speeches are theoretically categorized as a 'good thing' and in films, for example, they seem to have an enormous impact, the speech-maker using this opportunity to announce, 'I'm pregnant/in love/dying from an incurable disease/actually a transsexual.'

In reality, speeches are never major turning points in the course of our lives. Mostly they hold up the action as waiters can't get around refilling guests' glasses and you're stuck with nothing to drink until the speaker finally sits down. Don't be a speechifier unless asked to be so – i.e. when you're best man at a wedding.

...But first, just a few simple words

Spontaneous speeches lack flair. In fact they usually lack everything except alcohol-infused good intentions. Keep your counsel and let other guests make spectacles of themselves.

Whenever you're required to speak in public, appreciate the benefits of thorough preparation. Keep your remarks brief. The audience you're addressing will either be standing around (and shifting uncomfortably from one foot to another while you witter on for half an hour) or sitting at table and longing to continue the enjoyable chat they'd started just before you launched into your speech. Do your best to be amusing. Funny speeches are the most memorable (especially when made at the wrong time and place, like a funeral). But be careful: the obscene joke that had you guffawing last week might meet with a cooler response from a mixed audience. It's better not to tell jokes at all unless you're a stand-up comedian and this is how you make your living.

Write down what you plan to say but try not to read it out, no matter how nervous you're feeling: it will make your delivery terribly stilted and flat. Instead, take a little time to memorize the key points, practise saying them out loud a few times and include a couple of short pauses; you may need to allow your listeners a moment to absorb what you're saying and respond to it before moving on to the next point.

Making a good speech is a real art. As far as possible, let other people be the artists.

Divorce

Whether official (the couple were married) or unofficial (they were living together), the split's unlikely to be marked by a lavish celebratory party (although it has been known to happen). But it's still a significant moment in the lives of the two principal players and might need to be acknowledged as such. Even the most amicable split represents the sundering of a union between two people who'd once thought they had a permanent future together. That's not necessarily indicative of failure, but neither can it be taken as a mark of success. Many people who've experienced separation or divorce say the experience is akin to bereavement, so be prepared to offer sympathy and support if these are needed.

Do ask what you can do to help or whether one/other/both of the people involved would like to talk to you.

Don't be afraid to say that you don't know what to say. It's most likely that the separated/divorced person is looking for a listener, not a talker.

In the immediate aftermath of a split, sides are often taken. No matter how badly one of the parties involved has behaved – or so you've been told – resist the urge to ally yourself. Circumstances change, tempers cool, reason prevails. But your stand in favour of one person against another will be remembered. Acrimoniously separated couples have been known to get back together again; embarrassing for you if you've been too vocal in your criticisms of one of them.

Funerals

If you know the deceased or the bereaved well enough, telephone the family after the death and before the funeral to ask if you can help in any way – liaising with the undertaker, taking care of flowers, making sandwiches for visitors to the house. Death, especially when it's sudden or unexpected, can leave even the most capable of us incapacitated. Under these circumstances, while your services probably won't be needed, your thoughtfulness will be appreciated.

- Ask the bereaved would he/she like company or conversation. Don't force either if it's not required. Truly, some people do like to be left alone with their grief.
- If the funeral notice states that there are to be no flowers, respect this wish. If it suggests that donations to a certain charity would be welcomed, respect this also.
- Do attend the funeral ceremony if you possibly can.
- Be punctual. If you're late, stand at the back.
- Be discreet. Although funerals can often be large social gatherings, they're not parties and shouldn't be treated as such. Nor are they opportunities for networking or conducting business.
- Pay your respects to the bereaved briefly because a lot of other people will want to do the same. If you've more to say about the deceased, write a letter. A funeral line isn't the best

place for launching into long-winded reminiscences.
- ~ Sign the book of condolence as you're leaving.
- ~ Don't hang around gossiping for hours after the ceremony.
- ~ Only go to the bereaved's home if specifically invited. Don't presume that you'll be welcome.

After the funeral, send a card or letter to the bereaved. Write at the top of this 'no reply necessary'. A widow(er), son or daughter can receive hundreds of such letters – replying to all of them is an exhausting business, especially at such a difficult time. In the card/letter simply offer your sincerest condolences at the recipient's loss. Nothing more is required, there's no need to fill several pages. If you're not sure what to write, say just that – and then offer your sympathy. This really is an instance when it's the thought that counts most.

Grief takes a long time to pass. Even though the funeral was held a fortnight ago, your responsibilities aren't necessarily over. Keep a watching brief on someone who's been bereaved. Your support, though not needed at the time of death and burial, might make all the difference six months later when other friends have dropped away.

School Reunions

Quite why anybody would want to organize/attend one of these events remains one of life's great, unsolved mysteries. But there are lots of people who like the idea of revisiting their past and meeting childhood friends/old companions. If you go to a reunion, whether school/university/army/jail, be prepared.

Everyone will look older and, possibly, smaller than you remembered. Should the event be held in your old school, it too will somehow have shrunk. Expect to bump your head against at least one doorframe that used to tower above you.

Likewise, the staff will have diminished – in size and in number. They'll also be much nicer, more amusing, more human than they were when you spent time in the institution. You'll find this changed attitude towards you the most disturbing aspect of the reunion.

Keep any thoughts about other people's appearance to yourself. Announcing, 'God, but you've got very grey,' merits the reply, 'At least I've still kept my hair.' Your former companions have acquired lines, a broader waistline and an irritating tic of clearing their throats after every sentence. So have you.

At least one person present will have enjoyed a much better career than the rest of you ever expected. He'll also have lost his bottle-thick glasses, gained personal confidence and acquired a wife twenty years his junior. He will boast of all these attributes; you'll still remember him as a sports nerd who was never once selected, even for the school's worst football team.

One of the school's stars, captain of the hockey team, head of her year, most popular girl with the boys, will now be working as a packer at the supermarket where you do your weekly shop. She will have lost her looks, her self-confidence and, possibly, her husband in an acrimonious separation.

One woman will be a lesbian, one man will be serially divorced. One woman will have died and therefore be the subject of much reminiscence, one man will have been born again and try to talk you into attending his weekly Bible Study Group. One woman will have spent time in a convent, one man will have done time in a prison (if you raise the subject, he'll protest his innocence). And at least one person, expected to attend, won't do so. The rest of you are going to occupy a space somewhere between these extremes, now being middle-aged, middle-class and middle-management. Neither exaggerate nor downplay your achievements; they're much the same as those of all your school contemporaries.

Leave before the singing begins. And before you're asked to pledge 10 per cent of your earnings for the next five years towards rebuilding the school theatre.

Don't drink too much (whatever's served will be cheap, nasty and leave you with a crashing hangover). Otherwise you'll be tempted to revive allegiances and disputes that have lain dormant for the past thirty years. You'll also feel a powerful desire to tell that sweet old lady what a sadistic bitch she once was when a chemistry teacher or inform that dull accountant what a bully he used to be in the playground. It all happened a long time ago. If these incidents still retain a grip over you, what's needed is a good therapist, not a school reunion.

Christmas

Christmas is a time for families. It's also a time when families can be put through great strain and tempers go beyond being frayed to snapping completely. The traditional image of Christmas, purveyed to us through decades of sentimental films like *It's a Wonderful Life,* bears almost no relation to the reality. Having fondly regarded the occasion as a festive outpouring of love, you could find yourself in the middle of a long-simmering row between siblings or generations – or even be the cause/initiator of an argument. Resentments and feuds of ancient lineage are liable to resurface during Christmas, remarks made over the same period ten years ago are recalled, and slights – real or imaginary – revived.

Hesitate before designating yourself the local division of the UN peacekeeping force: you could be seriously injured in the crossfire. All families have their own dynamics: to paraphrase Tolstoy, each family bickers in its own unhappy way. You mightn't understand that way until it's too late to make an escape, or you could misinterpret its format and force. At Christmas, more than any other time of the year, don't start a row, keep out of any that are taking place and never take sides.

Christmas is primarily perceived as being 'for children'. Poor little things, in the weeks leading up to this occasion and particularly on the day itself, they're closely scrutinized for signs that a good time is being had. At intervals of less than five minutes, they'll be asked whether they're enjoying themselves. As a result of all this pressure from adults, they're liable to become fractious, tearful and exhausted – and it's still only six o'clock in the morning.

In fact, just like the rest of us, small children are liable to find Christmas a disappointment. At great cost and effort, you managed to find the Barbie your daughter wanted – but where are the pneumatic midget's twenty changes of outfit? Where her three-storey dream home? Where her pony and grooming kit? Your daughter wanted all of those as well. No wonder, before the end of breakfast, Barbie's been jettisoned in favour of loyal old Teddy. The more you build up the day in advance, the more it's likely to become replete with blighted hope. The best pleasures are always the most unexpected. This law applies as much to Christmas as to anything else.

How best to get through Christmas with a smile on your face? Keep yourself occupied. If, by mid-morning, you're already slumped on the sofa watching a black-and-white movie and clutching a tepid gin and tonic, the day won't go well. If, on the other hand, at around the same time you're standing in front of the kitchen sink peeling potatoes, it's going to be a triumph (unless, that is, you're mother to a large family and engage in this task every other day of the year). You needn't be a martyr (so no sighing as you bend to pick up fragments of crisps from the carpet), you do need to be busy as this leaves you less time to become embroiled in a family argument. Cook food, serve drinks, clear up wrapping paper – don't for a moment find yourself idle.

If you're spending Christmas away from your own home, even if it's with your parents or siblings, take responsibility for bringing plenty of the supplies. Again, the reason for this is that it'll make you an active contributor rather than a passive taker.

5. Socializing Outside the Home

Whether the location is McDonalds or a Michelin-starred restaurant, the same code of behaviour applies. Good behaviour is good behaviour, no matter where.

Punctuality

When meeting a friend or colleague in a bar, cafe or restaurant, elementary good manners require you to arrive punctually. While you might be excused, just about, for turning up at someone's home a little late – at least the host can always find something else to do there, like sit on a sofa and bitch to the other guests about your habitual tardiness – it's essential to arrive at the agreed time when meeting in a public venue. No one deserves to be left studying a restaurant menu for more than a minute; no matter how inventive the chef's prose, reading descriptions of food by yourself isn't half as much fun as eating it with someone else.

The only circumstance that trumps the above in terms of

discomfort is when you've arranged to meet someone *outside* a bar and are left waiting by the door. This experience reaches the nadir of humiliation when there's a steady downfall of rain.

An easy way to avoid being consistently kept waiting: when meeting anyone who has an established reputation for lateness, make up your mind to wait for a specific amount of time (ten minutes is good) and then, without any qualms of conscience, leave. Repeat as often as necessary until the latecomer learns new habits.

A late arriver should always apologize profusely. Keep the explanation for your delay brief; analysis of the M50's gridlock problems is unlikely to be greeted with much interest. In turn, an apology ought always to be accepted with good grace. Later you can take a solemn vow never to meet the tardy person again.

A further (and final) note on the waiting game. Whether the other person's a doctor, plumber or hairdresser, you're constantly making appointments to see people (or rather, for them to see you). Theoretically, as the paying client, by rights you should be allowed to run late. In reality, the professional who's taking your money will be the one with the lax attitude towards punctuality. Turn up ten minutes late for a hairdressing appointment and you'll be told you've missed your slot; turn up on time and you'll be asked to take a seat and thumb through three year-old copies of *Hello!* How you respond to this inversion of the natural laws of commerce depends on how important is the service you're seeking, and paying for. Walk out on a late hairdresser, for example, and you can always find someone else to look after your highlights. Walk out on a late plumber and your washing machine will continue to leak all over the kitchen floor.

Restaurants

ON ARRIVAL

When entertaining in a restaurant, the host ought to arrive at the table first. However, should you, in that role, be delayed, it's a good idea to ring the restaurant and leave an apologetic message for any guests who turn up before you. As a further gesture of consideration, you might like to ask that a waiter serve some drinks in your absence. This will have the effect of stifling potential irritation among the guests, as well as reassuring them that they haven't been stood up.

Guests who arrive before their host ought to resist the urge to order anything other than a glass of water. No matter how annoyed you feel at being left alone on the banquette, running up a hefty drinks tab is not a conciliatory gesture.

SEATING ARRANGEMENTS

These are for the host to decide, even if the guests arrive first. While it's not necessary to hover uncertainly around the table, you should avoid becoming too settled because without fail you'll be asked to move places when the rest of the party turns up. Organized hosts will prepare a seating plan and have this written out on a piece of paper. They'll also have booked next year's summer holidays, begun investing in a pension scheme by the age of twenty and arranged their CD collection in alphabetical order. The rest of us will frantically try to arrange seating arrangements as our guests arrive and we realize that at least two of them used to be lovers or business partners or both, but now don't speak to one another.

When there's no designated host or guest(s), then there are no longer any absolute rules. It used to be that women in restaurants were lined along the inside seats and men on the outside, but what if you're an all-male or all-female party? In most circumstances today, people should be allowed to sit wherever they like.

ORDERING

If there's a host, then the correct approach is to take your cue from him. Some hosts like to tell the waiter what the rest of their party is eating, others prefer you to state your own choice. Much as you might adore foie gras and lobster, it's better not to select these should they be much more expensive than every other item on the menu (and they will be).

If there's no host, order whatever you fancy but be prepared for disputes when the bill arrives (see below). It's helpful to agree how many courses you're all having before the waiter arrives at the table. Otherwise one member of the group (frequently the late arrival) will decide to order a starter even though nobody else is doing so. This means the rest of you must grow grumpy and/or drunk while waiting an additional half hour before your own food arrives.

Other ways of irritating the rest of the party include:

- Dithering hopelessly over the menu long after everyone else has made their choices.
- Changing your mind (and your order) when you hear what someone else is having – this is especially tiresome for the waiter who's already written down what he thought you wanted.
- Loudly regretting your choice when the food arrives and somebody else's order looks so much better than your own.
- Inviting yourself to taste food off other people's plates.

FOOD TALK

Consideration dictates that no one should begin eating a course until it has been served to all members of the party. On the other hand, if your meal looks like taking longer to appear than everybody else's, it's best to encourage the others to start. Otherwise their appetites will grow bigger as the food before them grows correspondingly colder.

Food ranks just below the weather as an interesting topic of conversation. No matter how grand the restaurant, what it serves is not a work of art but a work of industry. It deserves, therefore, to be eaten rather than discussed. The best way you can show your appreciation for the food on your plate is by consuming it. The worst way, especially for any diner seated next to you, is by talking about it.

WINE

As if it weren't bad enough that half the world's population have become garrulous gourmands (and there's nothing more boring than the monologue of a food bore), the other half now believe themselves to be wine connoisseurs. There's a particular snobbery about wine that has little to do with the drink being poured into your glass and a great deal to do with establishing the connoisseur's status. Wine buffs, by the way, are almost invariably male and treat their chosen area of expertise in the same way as do car experts or first-edition book collectors: by becoming tediously pompous on the subject. Connoisseurs never seem to notice that the rich density of their language, replete with reverential undertones below top notes of self-importance, does not noticeably improve the quality of the wine on which they are pontificating. 'I hope you like this,' will serve just as well as a five-minute sermon on the bottle, its label, contents and origin.

If the restaurant party has a host, you should leave the ordering of wine to him unless asked for your advice. In the latter circumstances, make a sensible choice – as with food, neither from the bottom nor the top of the list – and bear in mind that the mark-up on wine in these circumstances is, like the stench from a teenage boy's bedroom, frighteningly high.

Should you think the wine unsatisfactory (corked/gone off/no better than vinegar in a fancy bottle) get a second opinion from another member of the party before making your views known to the restaurant staff. And make them known in a pleasant fashion. While there's no need to be apologetic, aggression isn't necessary either – after all, the waiter didn't personally crush the grapes (you hope). As in so many other circumstances, politeness delivers better and faster results than rudeness.

PROBLEMS

The greatest risk when eating out at another person's expense is that something can – and will – go wrong:

- Your table is persistently neglected by the staff.
- The kitchen is having a bad night and the food is completely inedible.
- You're seated next to the (busy) lavatories.
- An adjoining party is riotously and offensively noisy.

Whatever the problem, try to remember that it's not the guest's role to complain – that job has already been allotted to the host who might or might not choose to speak his mind. Even if the experience is unforgettably awful, you must still behave as though the only memories you'll take away from the event will be glowing ones.

Hosts are entitled to complain, but preferably not in front of their guests and certainly not to the offensively noisy party at the next table, one of whom will turn out to be an amateur boxing champion. Hosts should make their complaint privately to the restaurant manager.

TABLE-HOPPING

Has the effect of making you look incredibly popular and/or important in a restaurant. It also has the effect of making the people with you look neither. Therefore, unless you particularly want to offend them, resist the urge to circulate around the room, call out remarks to another table or blow kisses towards a friend you've just noticed. A slight inclination of the head in the direction of someone you know might not seem like much but it'll be enough in the circumstances. If someone comes to your table, introduce them to the rest of the group and keep the conversation short. Otherwise everyone in your party will end up with a crick in their necks.

YOUNG CHILDREN IN RESTAURANTS

Parents often complain that restaurants are not child-friendly. By which they mean that these establishments don't always reduce both portions and prices, that the menu includes items unpopular among young consumers such as calves' liver, and that the kitchen is unwilling to serve chips with everything. Tomato ketchup will also not be available, with a jus of sun-dried tomatoes proposed as an alternative. This will fail to win the children's approval, just as they fail to win admirers among the rest of the restaurant's clientele, particularly once, having grown bored sitting at table, they begin to play a game of tag around the room. Children should be brought to restaurants only if they can sit quietly and eat an entire portion of broccoli without complaining once. Since neither of these feats is possible, they ought not to be brought to restaurants at all.

RESTAURANT STAFF

Everyone should be required to spend a month annually working as a waiter (or in some other service industry position) because it would lead to an immediate rise in manners among guests in a restaurant. Just because you're either affluent or lucky enough to have someone serve your food, this doesn't mean you can put the basic tenets of good behaviour on hold.

A fundamental obligation is to acknowledge service by saying please and thank you whenever you're offered or given assistance. Finger-clicking is never permissible nor is verbal rudeness. Waiting staff have their own code of revenge on offensive customers. You really don't want to know the details of this; just be aware that horrible things can happen to a plate of food before it's presented to a customer. Accordingly, it's best to mind your manners.

Notice how busy your waiter is before making additional demands on his time. If you're looking for something extra/exceptional, apologize for any potential trouble you've caused. Showing consideration will often lead to you getting better service, so everyone benefits. Ask the member of staff looking after you what he/she is called and use that name when making requests. If you're responsible for a large party, also tell the staff your name as this makes dealings with them much easier. They'll really appreciate your thoughtfulness, not least because it's so rarely found.

THE BILL

Even when invited to dinner by someone else, it's courteous to propose that you pay the bill or split its cost. This proposal ought to be turned down but in case it isn't, make sure always to bring a credit card with you. If your offer's refused, there's no need to persist. Presumably when your host extended the invitation, it was on the understanding that he/she had sufficient funds to cover the cost. But if you feel overwhelmed by the urge to make an immediate gesture of appreciation, propose buying a round of after-dinner drinks or even a bottle of champagne. Again, don't press the point if this suggestion is also spurned.

There still remains one way for you to show your gratitude: by reversing roles and in turn taking your host out to dinner.

Dining *à deux* with a friend? Both of you should offer to pay and then either split the cost or agree that one will take care of the bill on this occasion and the other do likewise whenever you next meet. This applies regardless of the diners' gender. A woman should not presume to have her meals bought by a man; this way lies post-dinner confusion about who's under an obligation to whom. No matter how often they're told otherwise, some men persist in imagining that because they've picked up the tab for a meal, women will want to show their appreciation for such generosity in a particular way. They won't, but a woman can avoid the risk of such confusion by paying her way.

When out to dinner with a group of friends, the easiest way to settle a bill is by equally dividing the total between all present. The most difficult way to settle a bill is by conducting a debate over who ordered the green salad and who had only one glass of wine with the main course. If you never go to a restaurant without your pocket calculator and love to subject the bill to itemized scrutiny, be prepared for a lifetime of solitary dining. Life really is too short to quibble over the cost of a side order of garlic bread.

The only exception to this rule is when one member of the party has agreed to assume the role of designated driver. Not only should this person not be expected to pay for any alcohol consumed by the rest of you, but furthermore he/she ought to be given a discounted bill in return for taking care of transport.

TIPPING

Some restaurants include a service charge on their bills, some don't. If you're eating in one that does, make sure the money really goes to the staff. Sometimes it just goes to enhance the owner's profits. It's particularly important to check this point when you're paying by credit or debit card. Your waiter will soon let you know if he receives the money or not. Even when he does, you may still like to leave some extra cash on the table.

Because the service charge is not a legal obligation, it's always your choice both whether and how much to give. Custom dictates that the average amount left for staff should be between 10 and 15 per cent of the total bill, but you're free to leave more or less, depending on what you think of the quality of service. And you're perfectly entitled to give nothing (receiving, in exchange, filthy looks from all the waiters as you depart). If the service was unremittingly lousy, here's an opportunity to express your opinion in a fashion that'll have a direct impact on those responsible.

Pub Etiquette

When out with a group of friends for the evening, be sure to cover the costs of your own drinks, either by buying them yourself or, better yet, by picking up the tab for a round. It's easy to gain a reputation for tight fistedness and, once acquired, hard to shake off.

When ordering at the bar, wait your turn to be served, even if the barman offers to help you before the person who's been desperately trying to gain his attention for the past ten minutes. Catching the eye of staff is a skill given to some people but not to others. (*Tip*: It helps if you're exceptionally tall, or a regular customer.) Should you be among those who always enjoy speedy service, don't do so at the expense of others because sooner or later, you'll get your comeuppance (like banging that tall head of yours on a low doorframe when leaving the bar).

6. Presents

Although social convention requires present-giving to take place on certain occasions (birthdays, Christmas, weddings, when you've had a fight with your partner and need to regain access to the house), the best time to offer a present is when it's least expected (leaving your partner to wonder whether the two of you did have a fight and he/she hadn't noticed). These are the gifts most likely to please the recipient, produced for no other reason than, 'I saw it and thought of you.' Try to give to friends and family on a regular basis and become known as the donor of a lot of small presents dotted throughout the year.

What's a Good Gift?

It's usually something the recipient would love to have, but probably not think of buying for him/herself because it's too expensive or too shamelessly self-indulgent. Make your present take the form of a treat; depending on your budget and on the interests of the person receiving it, this could be anything from a bottle of bath oil to a yacht moored in the Mediterranean.

SHORTAGE OF FUNDS

Don't allow your regular giving to become curtailed by financial constraints. This isn't a recommendation to run into debt. When money's in short supply, give what you can, not what you 'ought'. Lots of presents are within everyone's means and even if not lavish (a paperback novel, a scented candle, a picture of a yacht moored in the Mediterranean), they'll still be appreciated, especially as the recipient is likely to be aware of your economic circumstances. If you can't afford to spend a lot of money on your gift, spend a lot of time over it instead. Never apologize for only giving a little. If you really think your present is that inadequate, you shouldn't have given it in the first place.

THE INTERNET

It's a fabulous tool allowing you access to the global market. All around the world, like traders in an old-fashioned bazaar, retailers have their own websites where they lay out their wares for your perusal. All you'll need is a computer and a credit card. The internet site owner will do the rest for you, posting your present directly to the recipient. If you haven't bought from the company before, check two important details before making a purchase:

- That there's a security system in place to stop your credit card details being misused.
- That the internet retailer offers a returns service in case the present has to be sent back. Otherwise you could be stuck with a denuded credit card and a gift no one wants.

The Basics

Smart givers (the kind of people who are terrifyingly well organized, keep lists of what they've worn where and when, and never lose their car keys) will already know about the merit of maintaining a small present drawer. The presents themselves will tend to be of the generic rather than specific variety:

- Small picture frames.
- Pretty leather purses.
- Amusing key rings.
- Smart jars of honey or extra virgin olive oil (if one of the last of these, beware of letting it pass the use-by date).

When you're abroad and come across an attractive gift shop, or when your flight's delayed – as it inevitably will be – and there's time to kill at the airport, or if you simply find yourself browsing around town on a Saturday afternoon: these are all ideal moments to track down fresh additions to your present drawer.

IT'S THE THOUGHT THAT COUNTS

But does it? What about the occasions when you've been given a present that is wrong, wrong, wrong without any hope of it ever being right? Obviously, when handed a gift, you're obliged to consider the donor's thoughts and feelings. So *always* hide your disappointment/dismay/disgust and make sure you look delighted.

Soon afterwards follow your usual well-mannered procedure of writing/telephoning to say thank you. Now's the time to indicate, tactfully, that the present in question isn't completely right for you. In some instances (the likes of books or CDs) you can get away with telling a small fib and claiming to have bought yourself a copy already. Or, when it comes to items like clothes, you could suggest that the size, style or colour aren't suitable. Practised present-givers keep their receipts and have no trouble producing these so that goods can be exchanged for something else. They know that we all get things wrong sometimes and aren't offended when asked if an exchange is possible. The recipient can then skip off to the shops to buy a more satisfactory present and everyone's happy with the outcome.

Don't, under any circumstances, give as a birthday present something you were given for your birthday, or offer to a newly married couple one of the gifts received at your own wedding.

Should you hand on a present, try to make sure the original donor doesn't hear what you've done in case offence is taken. But if the donor does find out what's happened, confess at once (as you should always do when found to be in the wrong) and explain that, much as you appreciated the thought behind the present, it really wasn't going to get much use. So you gave it to someone who was really grateful.

Dislike the idea of giving away presents to other people, even when you don't want to keep them yourself? There is an excellent alternative and that is to donate unloved gifts to a charity. Many of these have shops that are forever on the lookout for items that they can sell to raise money for their cause.

GIFT TOKENS

Stumped for an idea? It's true, there really are some people who challenge even the most experienced present-giver's abilities. The solution: a gift token. Not strikingly original, but so what? Especially if your only alternative is turning up empty-handed. It doesn't have to be a book token (although, that said, there's almost nothing nicer than to browse in a bookshop knowing you've someone else's money to spend). Most shops offer tokens for their goods, whether they're car spare parts or a series of facials. And if the shop doesn't actually have tokens, it will certainly be able to provide you with the equivalent: a credit note, which you can then give as the present.

Try to choose a token or credit note appropriate to the recipient's interests. So, not red lingerie for your husband or a drill bit for your girlfriend. Unless, of course, these accurately reflect their personal tastes.

The most important thing to remember when handing over a gift token is to make it look as attractive as possible because frankly, a credit note, no matter what its other attractions, is never going to be an object of great beauty. Dress the present up by putting it into a big bag or box, smothered in lots of tissue paper and decked out with ribbons and bows. The result will be much more appealing than a plain envelope.

SIX CONSISTENTLY GOOD GIFT TOKENS
- Books (there really is a book out there to suit every interest).
- CDs.
- Beauty treatments for women (and for more and more men too).
- Clothes (especially if made from silk or cashmere).
- Dinner in an expensive restaurant (when you're buying this, make sure to include the cost of drink and also some sort of tip for the staff).
- An annual magazine subscription.

PRESENTS THAT, DESPITE BEST INTENTIONS, CAN BE OPEN TO MISINTERPRETATION
- A team of professionals to clean the house (shorthand for: you are a slattern).
- Membership to a gym (shorthand for: you are overweight).
- Expensive face cream (shorthand for: you are covered in wrinkles).
- Itsy-bitsy lingerie (shorthand for: you are a tart, or at least I wish you would be).
- For women, anything to do with cooking (shorthand for: you belong in the kitchen).

WRAPPING PRESENTS

It is a truth universally acknowledged that a large bow tied around anything will make it look better. Work on the premise that presentation is all – or as near as dammit – because how a gift looks can make all the difference to how it's received. Also understand that the more modest the gift, the better its wrapping ought to be (although this can lead you to spend more money on the presentation than the present).

None of which means you have to smother your presents in a garish display of tinsel and glitter. Think smart rather than gaudy. Smartness begins with having the right equipment, such as a good pair of scissors and a roll of Sellotape – double-sided is best because then it can be hidden from view.

In addition, keep a couple of rolls of ribbon in stock at home, either in boldly contrasting or in complementary colours; two different shades of ribbon (and in two different thicknesses)

ONE CAN *NEVER* HAVE TOO MANY SMARTIES, AND THE PURE CASHMERE WRAPPING PAPER IS LOVELY

always look great together. Learn how to tie a bow because the pre-tied, self-adhesive ones, while practical, aren't inspiring. And don't forget the old trick of running the sharp edge of a scissors blade down the length of ribbon to make it curl. Try to save any ribbon that comes on gifts you are given; press this under a warm iron to get rid of creases before rolling it up and storing it with your other present materials for another occasion.

EXTRAS

There are people who include loose bits of glitter, little stars and the like, when wrapping their gifts. In theory this is a lovely idea and adds to the attractiveness of the presentation, until some-one – usually the person who's been given the gift – has to pick bits of glitter out of the carpet for much of the following day.

GOOD PLANNING

No matter what your feelings on the subject, it's never too early to start buying Christmas presents. One advantage to this approach is that it spreads the cost over several months, giving the cheerful, if erroneous, impression of hitting your pocket less hard. By starting early, you'll also be much calmer than you would trying to get everything done in late December. You're therefore more likely to make clear-headed decisions. Accepted, there's something absurdly over-organized about stocking up on Christmas gifts in the spring (who's to know whether you'll still be talking to all the people on your list nine months later?) but from September onwards you can start to buy – by which time you'll have drawn up your provisional list of recipients.

Helpful tip: Always buy a couple of extra Christmas presents. Without fail, someone will turn up over the festive season with a gift for you, and you'll have nothing to offer in return. Your reciprocal present needn't be much and it needn't be fancy but it needs to be something: a little beaded purse; a leather-bound notebook; even a box of smart writing pencils. These are the kind of items that, in any case, you keep for emergencies in your ever-handy present drawer. They're your social safety net. And if, by some chance, they aren't needed, they can go back into the drawer for another occasion.

Classic Presents

PERFUME

Only give this if you're completely confident of the recipient's taste. Otherwise, brace yourself for a receipt request so your present can be exchanged (see above). Scent is extremely personal and you're as likely to make the wrong choice as the right one. Plus, what you think of as an attractive fragrance might be considered tarty, or old-fashioned, or even downright disgusting by the person getting it.

Many women view presents of perfume in the same light that men do gifts of socks or ties: as an unimaginative stand-by for people who couldn't be bothered to take much trouble. Their appreciation will reflect this opinion. Everyone's bathroom contains at least two bottles of perfume given as presents and never used. These are easily identified by the thick layer of dust covering their surfaces.

The other risk with gifts like perfume is that, having met with approval once, they tend to be given over and over again. Every Christmas you've presented your mother with the same bottle of Chanel No. 5 because she once expressed a fondness for it. Continuing to give her the same thing annually implies you think she has a predictable character, while she'll think you're boringly repetitive.

FLOWERS

Are probably the most common present, especially from guests to hosts. That's 'common' as in frequent rather than vulgar, although the latter can sometimes be the case, particularly if you bought the bouquet from a petrol station forecourt or in the supermarket because then it'll be an uninspiring bunch of mixed blooms, long past their sell-by date and coated in a film of grime.

When choosing flowers to bring as a gift, think of the place in which they'll be displayed; their design and colour ought to harmonize with the surroundings. Consider also your hosts' tastes and choose accordingly. Think about how best to make an impact with your offering – by arriving with either a lot or a little, either a huge cluster of lilies or a single orchid. The exotic will always be noticed but even the ordinary can look wonderful provided it comes in sufficient quantities. There's something stunning about several dozen tulips, for example, or an enormous clutch of freesias. In small amounts, on the other hand, both appear rather pitiful. Devote a little time to personalizing your present. Instead of leaving them smothered in cheap plastic, wrap the flowers in some coloured tissue paper tied with silk ribbon holding a handwritten card.

Despite all this effort, you could find the recipient, when presented with a bouquet, saying 'how lovely' in a distinctly unenthusiastic tone of voice. The problem's simple: whoever was given the flowers now has to find a container and fill it with water to hold your gift. Many florists arrange for the stems of a bouquet to be sealed in a small plastic bag of water, so see if this can be done. Or take along a vase with the promise that next time you'll bring the flowers to go into it.

Best of all, why not send flowers either before or after seeing the person who'll be getting them? If the former, include a note saying how much you're looking forward to your meeting. If the latter, your thank-you note can accompany the bouquet. Just make sure you get it the right way round and don't send flowers saying how much you're looking forward to seeing someone after you've done so.

ALCOHOL

Is always an excellent present, provided you approach it with the correct spirit of generosity.

Champagne will never fail to meet with approval. While the cost is liable to be high, this ought to be *real* champagne from a reputable house and not some over-fizzed New World imitation. If you're going to dinner, one bottle will do; two or more should be brought when you're staying overnight. Also welcome is a good bottle of whiskey/gin/vodka should you know your hosts are spirit drinkers. And if you've a favourite tipple, why not bring that along (bearing in mind you're going to be the only one who appreciates the merits of a cream-based pineapple liqueur).

Wine is more of a problem, especially if the recipient's a bit of a buff, as most people now seem to be. You can look like a fool by turning up with an inexpensive bottle bought from the local supermarket, and seeing this decisively put away on a cupboard shelf marked 'For Cooking Purposes Only'. Take advice from the experts and remember that it's better to arrive with a single bottle of good wine than with several of poor quality. If you've been staying with friends or family and have become familiar with their tastes, why not contact a local wine merchant afterwards and arrange to have a few bottles sent over to them?

Finally, if you've brought wine, be prepared for your gift to remain unopened in your presence. It's annoying to bring vintage claret to a party and then be served something nasty from a former Soviet republic but that's the recipient's prerogative. All you can do is to swallow your pride (along with as little as possible of the stuff being poured out) before consoling yourself with a decent drink when you're back home.

Four Special Present Ideas

EDIBLES

Although they tend to be given mostly around the Christmas season, gifts of food or drink are welcome at any time of year, especially if they're luxury treats. Go to the trouble of making up your own basket or hamper of goodies – its contents will invariably be more interesting than those available from specialist companies. A great source for hamper materials are the farmers' markets that have sprung up around the country. Here you'll discover delicious foods that are distinctive, organic or home-made or possibly all three. In any case, they certainly won't be standard supermarket fare. Speaking of which, avoid giving as a present anything encased in cellophane; the stuff looks cheap, it's a nuisance to dispose of and it doesn't allow edibles such as fresh fruit or cheese to breathe properly. Likewise minimize the inclusion of pre-packaged items like boxes of biscuits. And dispense with the obvious; everyone gets far too many presents of Christmas cake and some of it will still be kicking around in mid-June. One last point: if your present has a limited shelf life, tell the recipient immediately so that it isn't left to fester in a kitchen cupboard.

TRAVEL

For men and women alike, surprise trips make a wonderful present. And the range of options is wider than you'd think. There are the regular favourites like a day at the local health spa with a series of treatments, but don't forget all the sporting options: a private box for the afternoon at a racecourse; a round of golf at one of the more exclusive (and pricey) clubs; dinner and a night at the dog track (and throw in a few betting tickets while you're at it); a pair of tickets for one of the Six Nations matches or a Premier Division football game.

Alternatively, instead of sport, think culture: most theatres around the country now sell gift vouchers, so how about a couple of those; or tickets for one of the National Gallery's visiting exhibitions; or a pair of seats at a charity film première (plus admission to the after-screening party, of course).

A night (or two) in a hotel will certainly win favour. Everybody loves the idea of running away from daily life and there's nothing nicer than staying in a hotel where someone else takes care of all tasks. This present needn't be as expensive as it first appears; hunt around on the internet and you'll quickly find that hotels are always offering special deals. Or get on the phone and barter a good rate. Just remember to check the recipient's availability of dates before you book the room.

SEQUENTIAL PRESENTS

The more affluent giver might like to think of presents that are spread over a period of time – that way you'll be remembered for longer. Possibilities include a set of six manicures or facials booked one per month. Rather than giving your present all at once, consider it as being on a slow time-release, whether a year's membership of a book club (with new books being sent throughout the twelve months), a magazine subscription or a standing order with the local florist to deliver a fresh bouquet for a certain number of weeks.

GOOD MEMORIES

The perfect present to give when you haven't much money to spend. Buy a disposable camera, bring it to the party, temporarily transform yourself into Mario Testino, take lots of lovely pictures, have these developed (promptly – *not* six months after the event), arrange them in a smart album, write amusing captions and present the result to a delighted party-giver who'll then tell you this is the best present – ever.

Other Gifts

BOOKS ON TAPE/CD
Are a fabulous gift for anyone who's a regular traveller. Pick either an already well-loved work or a classic rather than a book that's enjoying transitory popularity – you want your present to be used again and again.

LOTTERY TICKETS
Yes, the recipient might end up winning a fortune but much more probably he/she will be left with a worthless piece of paper. So, better not – unless you like the idea of your present being thrown into the rubbish bin five minutes after it has been given.

ELECTRICAL GOODS
If you've a bit of extra cash to spend, small gadgets make surprisingly successful presents for everyone, regardless of age or gender. These are items such as miniaturized radios that can be pinned onto a jacket, listened to anywhere and make the user feel like a member of the secret service. Or those convenient personal organizers that are hardly larger than a credit card but can store your diary, address book, etc. Just check that it's not too complicated to use or that the keypad/screen isn't so tiny that a magnifying glass is needed to use it.

EXTRA-ADDED VALUE
For example, if you're going to give someone a good bottle of white wine or champagne, encase it in one of those freezer chillers that are so useful. No one ever has enough of them, so your thoughtfulness will still be remembered long after the

wine is drunk. Similarly, when you're bringing a plant to a friend, put it into a smart ceramic pot (instead of the horrible plastic one it has been sold in). Even if the plant doesn't last a week, at least another part of your present will.

Presents For ...

CHILDREN

We're often inclined to buy presents that we think children *should* want instead of those they'd actually like. Typically, we'll buy a set of Beatrix Potter books on the basis that every child ought to have these. The youthful recipient will think otherwise. Discuss with parents what their offspring would actually enjoy, while bearing in mind that parents too are inclined to engage in a form of improving censorship and could, in turn, propose Beatrix Potter.

Don't give children anything educational – it'll make you feel virtuous and make them feel ungrateful.

Only buy clothes for children when you're abroad and can visit fantastic shops that aren't available at home. Check in advance about sizes; you'll have some trouble exchanging clothes when the shop is on the other side of the Atlantic Ocean.

Recognize that gifts to children will, within six months, be either broken or discarded as no longer of any interest (or, in the case of clothes, too small to be worn anymore). Don't, therefore, turn up in a year's time enquiring what happened to that expensive train set you gave.

For godchildren, why not set up a bank account into which you can pay some money (no matter how little) whenever you've spare cash. For legal reasons, the child's parents will have to open the account, otherwise those suspicious people in the Department of Finance might believe this is just a tax-avoidance dodge. After that it becomes your responsibility. Fix an age when your godchild will be allowed access to the account's contents, hoping that by then:

- ❧ He/she will have learnt basic financial sense and not blow the whole lot in a week.
- ❧ Bank interest rates will have increased.

Of course, setting up an account doesn't exempt you from giving presents to godchildren on relevant occasions like birthdays and Christmas.

Particularly with young children, brace yourself for the possibility that the box in which your present came will turn out to be more appealing than its contents.

TEENAGERS

Only one thing will make a teenager happy and that's cash. They can use this to make their own mistakes, a thing that teenagers invariably do.

PEOPLE IN HOSPITAL

Unless you know the patient plans to run a little bedside business as a florist, no flowers please. If you want to bring something living, make it a pot plant. Offer to drop this round to the patient's home at a later date; even people who arrive in hospital with barely a toothbrush somehow, before their departure from the ward, manage to accumulate the most extraordinary number of possessions.

Think pampering treats, as hospitals can be quite tough places: an extra-soft pillow; a light blanket; some really luxurious hand cream; a padded eye-mask; a bowl of strawberries or other soft fruit. How about providing a little CD player, if only on loan, together with some soothing albums to play (the only alternative entertainment usually being the flicker of the television in a corner of the room). Before rushing to buy a stack of newspapers or magazines, check which ones the patient already has – there are only so many copies of this week's *Hello!* that any of us will ever want to own.

When visiting maternity hospitals, don't bring something for the baby. The newborn will already be smothered with presents (and be far too young to appreciate any of them). Focus on the new mother who, having just gone through labour, is probably in need of some extra special care and consideration. This could be anything, from a voucher for a post-natal massage to the news that you've popped half a dozen prepared meals into her freezer for her return home.

FRIENDS/FAMILY LIVING OVERSEAS

They may have left the country because they hated it and never want to see or hear from the place again. But much more likely they love to keep in touch. Help them to do so with the gift of a year's subscription to one of the national newspapers (or its on-line equivalent), or whichever is their relevant weekly regional paper. Think about posting over a set of magazines that'll provide a good overview of what's been happening back home.

Food parcels are always welcome but check in advance that the country to which it's being delivered won't confiscate the contents at customs. Throw into the parcel some things that, while not necessarily made for the sophisticated adult palate, exude childhood nostalgia, like a jar of Marmite, some Twinings tea or a box of traditional shortbread.

Although we can talk on the telephone or send emails to anyone across the world, it's still possible to feel out of touch. Give some thought to a present that helps to re-establish the connection, like a video in which friends and relations send personal messages and fill in details of their news. Or a photograph album that tells the story of what's taken place in your life during the past year. And don't just send these at Christmas when we're all frantically contacting one another. Pick a quiet period when your present will arrive as a delightful surprise.

FRIENDS BACK HOME

Helpful tip: Limoncella does not travel well. Neither do any of the other sweet and sticky drinks that taste so delicious when you sip them late at night on holiday.

Before buying a gift while overseas, ask yourself: how will the miniature leather camel that doubles as a toothpick holder look in someone else's home? If you're not confident of the answer, return the item to the shop shelf.

Look out for items that are available at home, but cost less elsewhere, whether it be drink or small electrical goods. With the latter, you'll need to check that their wattage/voltage/whatever allows them to be used here. The same is also true for the likes of videos and DVDs.

PEOPLE WHO'VE MOVED INTO A NEW HOUSE

Visit the place first so you can see what its new occupants actually want or need rather than what you think they might like. If a preliminary visit isn't possible, don't be afraid to ask what they would like. Think practical – a kettle or an iron or even an ironing board. Moving house is incredibly expensive and when people have just done so (especially if it's their first home) they often don't have any money left even for the most basic necessities. An ironing board mightn't seem a stylish present to you, but it's going to be much more useful to new householders than the set of six sherry glasses you had in mind.

EMPLOYEES

There are two specific times when you must produce a gift for employees:

- Christmas.
- For work above and beyond the call of duty.

And, it's worth noting, these are also the two occasions when you needn't worry about what to give: a straightforward present of money will be perfectly acceptable.

AND FINALLY
If you still don't know what to give, then give nothing. Don't waste money buying a present just for the sake of it. If you haven't had the time or opportunity to find something right, offer some kind of IOU – a smart bunch of flowers, for example, with an apologetic note attached promising to produce the real gift at a future date.

7. Special Interest Groups

The old notion of children being seen and not heard has long since fallen out of vogue. Today, even though they have yet to acquire rudimentary social skills, children are likely to be both visible and vocal. This means that whenever you come into contact with them, while their appearance can give a deceptive impression of mature civility, their manners are still going to be at an embryonic stage of development. They won't yet have learnt to resist interrupting adult talk and they're inclined to believe that whatever subject interests them – the new Gameboy, Barbie's latest outfit change – will be just as fascinating for everyone else. Worst of all, they suffer from the combination of a short attention span and a weak grasp of irony.

Children

YOUR OWN CHILDREN
Are not necessarily as fascinating as you imagine them to be. First-time parents are usually guilty of behaving as though no one else has ever gone through a similar experience.

While your children mean a great deal to you, they probably won't occupy quite so large a place in the hearts of your friends.

Talk about them only when asked to do so, and then keep it brief.

Think carefully before introducing children, either in conversation or in company. Oddly enough, while young Seán seems to be his mother's only concern when he's out of her sight, she displays absolutely no interest in him when he's actually with her. Over Sunday brunch in a popular restaurant, his parents are so busy talking to their friends about his future schooling, that they haven't noticed how young Seán is driving every other customer in the place insane by running unrestrained between tables.

As a parent, you've quickly grown accustomed to your children's habit of pulling off shelves anything within their reach; other shoppers, and the staff of your supermarket won't know about this. They won't be used to hearing the question 'Why Mummy?' asked repeatedly and in a steadily escalating tone of voice. Nor, unlike you, will they have trained themselves to ignore little Emily's outbreaks of petulance whenever she doesn't get her own way. Who'd have imagined someone so small could produce that much noise?

You might want your children to grow up unfettered and free from restraint. Outside the home, however, they ought to be subject to the same conventions as anyone else. All of us have to curb our natural impulses when in public; the sooner this lesson is learnt, the better for everybody.

By the way, all talk of nannies, au pairs, childcare, crèches, etc. is also, as a rule, of limited interest and has been known to bring otherwise excellent dinner parties to an early conclusion.

OTHER PEOPLE'S CHILDREN

Except for their parents, no one is ever allowed to complain about or correct children. They're like your best friend's awful boyfriend; regardless of what you really think about him, as far as she's concerned, he's perfectly wonderful and you're not going to disagree. Parents are perpetually blind to their off-springs' failings or else forever tolerant of them. Follow their example. Find fault in a child and you could find yourself before a human rights' tribunal in Brussels.

This advice is particularly applicable to the children of friends. Try to remember their names, ages and interests even though the last of these change with bewildering speed; prepare to find yourself being corrected by a jaded five-year-old. Friends' children are often drafted in to help at parties, collecting glasses or handing around food; if met under these circumstances, make sure you thank them for their help, avoiding any hint of condescension in your tone. Discretion in the company of children is recommended; remember that when you have gone home, they will repeat to their parents whatever they saw and heard among the guests. You don't want to be responsible for initiating the query, 'Daddy, what's bestiality?'

If you find all this impossible and the thought of children at a social gathering seems intolerable, it is probably best if you become the one who, on such occasions, is neither seen nor heard.

Teenagers

Are quite different from children and can be openly criticized. Their own parents will certainly do so at every opportunity and you're entitled to follow this example. Teenagers are a strange breed, a law-unto-themselves and certainly not human as the rest of us understand that term. This is of course a phase, but one that gives the impression of going on indefinitely. After what feels like a life sentence of dirty clothing, untidy bedrooms, unhealthy diets in which a packet of crisps is perceived as having nutritional value, and sentences composed of the single mumbled word 'Dunno' – suddenly a pleasant, responsive human being emerges from the grubby chrysalis of adolescence.

In the meantime, the rest of us should keep our tempers when in the company of a teenager; losing it only confirms that all adults are irrational creatures obsessively preoccupied with making sure the dishwasher's been stacked properly. Never try to understand the teenage mind; owing to hormonal imbalances, it works on a different system to our own. It is also inadvisable to attempt conversation with teenagers because they perceive us adults as being incapable of understanding their own concerns. Conversation will also expose how hopelessly out of touch you are with current trends in clothing, music, language and places to hang around on a Saturday afternoon.

Lead by example. Show teenagers through your own actions and speech how you'd like them to behave. Naturally they'll ignore you, but don't be discouraged. Even if – as will almost inevitably be the case – they continue to act as appallingly as ever, at least you have the consolation of knowing that you tried. To paraphrase the Olympic Games maxim, where teenagers are concerned, it's not the winning that counts, it's managing to survive the encounter with your dignity intact.

Note to teenagers: Of course you're right. Your younger brothers and sisters are boring and childish and your parents are just pathetic. So too are all their friends. Nobody understands you or the problems you're going through at the moment. You're entitled to dress entirely in black, listen to heavy metal played at full volume, slam every door and not say what time you'll be coming home tonight. Now that's all been agreed, would you mind stacking the dishwasher – properly?

Posh People

And all the other old-style grandees out there. Don't be disconcerted by titles – just think of them as being quirky variants of your own Mr/Ms/Mrs/whatever. And don't be worried about making mistakes, especially since the strata of those funny old aristocratic titles are often incredibly complicated. Thankfully, charm, courtesy and consideration matter much more in our society. Display an abundance of this triumvirate and your failure to have memorized the contents of *Burke's Peerage* will be of no consequence.

Bear in mind that lots of peers don't use their titles any longer and whenever this is the case neither should you. If someone's introduced as Joe Bloggs, for example, that's the name by which you address him, not the Earl of Bloggs, even though this might be his formal title. You'll appear pathetically snobbish calling him 'My Lord' when everyone else is talking about/to Joe. Treat this as a When-in-Rome occasion.

Regard all titles – whether attached to an archbishop or archduchess (or just an arch friend) – the same way you would a barrage of unfamiliar knives and forks; observe what other people present are doing and follow their example. You might discover that Joe Bloggs, who's an elderly man, prefers to be addressed formally. In other words, when using his name in the course of conversation, you should say Lord Bloggs rather than Joe. There's nothing necessarily wrong with this approach: lots of untitled people, especially if they grew up in a different era, would rather be called Mr Bloggs on initial acquaintance and not have their first names bandied about by someone they've never met before.

Good manners dictate that you let the other person choose how he/she wants to be addressed because you'll want the same courtesy extended to you. No matter how ridiculous you find titles (and yes, frankly, there's something inherently absurd and irrational about them), save that argument for another time.

Celebrities

And everyone else you might meet who is famous/successful/ popular/wealthy. You amble into what had promised to be just another pleasant dinner party and, oh my God! There's Tom Cruise and he looks amazing (if about six inches shorter than you'd been led to expect from *Mission Impossible II*) and he's sitting in the chair next to yours.

Under these circumstances, the first and most important rule is to avoid uttering, 'Oh my God!' or any other expression that denotes shock, agitation or the incipient onset of heart failure – Tom Cruise doesn't usually play a medic so he might have trouble identifying your symptoms of catatonic shock. No matter how great the struggle, contain your excitement. Instead, like A.E. Housman, proclaim, 'Be still, be still, my soul,' and take your seat. Introduce yourself to Mr Cruise; just because you've seen him before – and doesn't he look a lot taller on screen? – it won't follow that he knows your name. You'll probably find that he then introduces himself. Curb the temptation to nudge him in the ribs and say that of course you know who he is. Likewise no asking for autographs or insights into his marriage with Nicole Kidman. ('Was the fact that you were shorter than her the start of your problems, Tom?') Don't try to discuss anything personal – about his life or yours – and don't expect this to be the start of a long and beautiful friendship. You will never see the man again.

You could be tempted to veer in the opposite direction and behave as though you've never heard of the celebrity who's just been introduced. 'What did you say your name was? Tom

Cruise? No, I don't think I've seen any of your films. Are you really tall enough to be an actor?' – that kind of thing. You might think you're being refreshingly blasé; he'll just think you're being standard-issue rude. But if you really never go to the cinema and haven't therefore witnessed all those occasions when Tom Cruise breaks into a slight sweat while trying to restore justice and democratic values to a troubled world, be honest enough to say so and give him the opportunity to explain his craft (now, that should be a long conversation). Likewise Madonna and her music, Tiger Woods and his golf swing, the Queen and her finely honed skill of opening new hospital wings.

One last thing: never hog a celebrity. If he/she is that famous there'll be other people itching to spend a few minutes basking in the same glow. Don't be greedy. Oh, and have the decency to wait until Tom Cruise has left the room before remarking how short he is.

8. The Workplace

Understandably, employers judge us by how well we behave at work; stack those supermarket shelves in a shoddy way and you needn't expect anything other than a negative assessment of your long-term prospects with the company. By the way, arguing that you're not being paid enough to do the task any better is no argument at all. The response you'll get to this is always be the same. You don't like the job? Feel free to walk.

Life in the Workplace

Ask yourself a simple question: do I see the work that I'm now doing as a career or a job? Whether collecting dustbins or running a multi-national corporation, the question is still relevant and the choice is still yours. Decide as soon as possible which of these two you want your work to be and strategize accordingly. If what you're doing is no more than a job, then your primary incentive's likely to be any income earned from it. In that case, ask yourself: is this really the best means of earning as much money as possible? It's quite possible that another job, even one offering no more personal satisfaction, would pay better. Investigate the possibilities.

On the other hand, if you're thinking in terms of a career, then money – while still important – won't be your primary motivation. Moving forward to achieve specific goals takes precedence. Regular assessment of what you want from your job is a useful exercise because the conclusions reached will help to make your work more satisfying, make the place where you work more pleasant, and make you more contented with your fellow workers.

Be enthusiastic, although within reason. Otherwise you'll drive the people working with you completely crazy (i.e. curb any tendencies to bounce cheerily around the office at eight o'clock on a Monday morning). While it's true that nobody's going to derive enormous personal satisfaction from checking the validity of health insurance claims, you're much less likely to find this job intolerable if you bring a dash of vigour to the enterprise. That's another important reason for staying enthusiastic; it means you do the job better. After all, what's your alternative? Being miserable. And who wants that?

All whingeing is dreary. Complaining about your work (that you've too much, that it's repetitive, that you're stuck in a rut) is especially boring. Don't do it. Instead, pull yourself together and sort out whatever's the problem.

Be punctual, again without taking this to absurd extremes. Don't feel you have to arrive first or be the last to leave the office. These days both can give the impression that you're taking too long to get your work done. They also suggest to fellow workers that you're trying to suck up to the bosses (not a good way to encourage office camaraderie).

APPEARANCE

If you've been given a uniform, keep it clean and tidy. That way you'll look better, and feel better too. Uniform or not, you won't make a good impression on your bosses if you turn up for work

ARE THOSE **COMPANY** PAPER CLIPS
MISS MURPHY

looking slovenly. They'll come to the conclusion that you're not interested in the job – and they'll probably be right (in which case, what are you doing there anyway?).

While many jobs don't require employees to wear an official uniform, there'll still be an unofficial dress code. Discreetly check out what this is and, regardless of your personal preferences, conform to it. Frankly, when was the colour of your tie or the length of your skirt worth an argument with the office superior over what is/isn't 'appropriate' for work? The bigger the organization employing you, the more probable that conformity of appearance will be expected among members of staff. Rebel against this at your peril; the corporate environment rarely welcomes mavericks. That's why so many Richard Branson clones prefer to start their own businesses. If you want to stand out from your fellow workers, try to do so through the quality of your work rather than because of the colour of your hair or the piercings in your nose.

Never overdress at work – you're in the office, not at a cocktail party. Keep accessories to a minimum, likewise make-up, bright colours, strong prints, etc. Bear in mind Sigourney Weaver's rebuke to her personal assistant in *Working Girl*: 'Let's rethink the jewellery.' It's a good idea to devise your own professional wardrobe: clothes that have been bought only for wear in the workplace. These will be functional, hard-wearing and an accurate reflection of how seriously you take your job. Clothes expressing any other aspect of your personality can – and should – be saved for times when you're not at work.

TIDINESS

Used to be next to godliness. On the job, you'll find it located beside common sense. Tidy your workplace regularly; the job will be much easier if you can find what you want when you want it, whether on your desk or in your locker. Yet again, it'll also impress your bosses (notice, by the way, how heads of big corporations always sit behind immaculate desks, not so much as a pencil out of place). Personalize your workplace by all means, but in moderation. Not the hundreds of pink teddy bears, potted busy Lizzies or postcards sent by friends holidaying in Lanzarote. All these have a habit of becoming a messy distraction. Spare a thought for the feelings of fellow-workers. Amazingly, some people might take offence at the breasts of last week's Page Three girl.

At work as at home, learn the art of discarding whatever's not necessary. If you haven't looked at a file for a month, either store it in the communal office system or throw it away altogether. Despite computers, all of us still accumulate far too much paper, most of it a duplication of material that's easily accessible elsewhere. If there's an additional copy of a document in the building, either in a cupboard or on disc, take a deep breath and dump your own. Organize a personalized filing system and keep this up-to-date by staying back late once a month or utilizing a quiet lunch break.

And don't forget recycling – use both sides of every sheet of paper. It's beneficial to the environment and it saves the company money.

EATING AT YOUR DESK

Never a good look. Weeks later, you'll discover a sliver of chicken tikka lodged between the pages of a file you were consulting at the time. A smear of mayonnaise will also, inevitably, run down the side of your desk and onto your tie; that won't look so impressive at your two o'clock meeting. Furthermore, there's the small, but not unimportant, question of hygiene. Unless you're planning to hose down and sterilize the entire room after eating, food in the work environment risks leaving behind germs – for you and for others. There are also lingering odours. Why should anyone working in the vicinity have to smell your heavily vinegared fries? Finally, it's a good idea to take a couple of breaks from your job during the course of the day. No matter how frantically busy, you'll work better and with a clearer head after taking some time out from the routine. Lunch hour is an ideal opportunity for this.

PHONE MANNERS

Always answer a ringing phone. So you're managing director of the company – does that mean you've lost the power of speech? No matter how high or low your professional status, you should want the organization that's paying your salary to do well; one obvious way to encourage this is by answering every call promptly and politely. Don't assume it's someone else's job; an unanswered phone represents potentially lost business. If the caller's looking for another person, take a message and make sure it reaches the intended destination.

Take a vow never to leave your place of work without all the day's calls answered. The excuse that you've been busy is worthless. Do you think the rest of us spend the hours from nine until five having our nails manicured? Busyness isn't exclusive to you. Everyone's busy but some people are also organized and an even smaller number of them are considerate. Make sure you belong to the last category; it'll be to your professional advantage. After all, who would you rather do business with – someone who replies to your email promptly or someone who doesn't bother?

Make phone calls yourself. It's the essence of bad manners to have your secretary ring somebody and then enquire, 'Will you hold for so and so?' The only response to this question is, 'No,' followed by the sound of the phone being hung up. Who, after all, has rung whom?

During a telephone conversation, try not to put someone on hold unless it's absolutely necessary and then do so only for the shortest time. If the incoming call's urgent and looks like taking some time, return to the original one, make your apologies and offer to ring back soon.

Unless it's a conference call, talking on the speaker phone is a no-no: pick up the receiver. If it is a conference call, introduce everyone else present in the room to the outside caller and make sure each of them says a few words to identify his/her voice.

You're going to be away from work for some time? Tell the receptionist, leave a message to that effect on your voicemail and inform colleagues. That way callers won't be left wondering why they haven't heard back from you for the past fortnight.

When you call someone at work and have to leave a message, do so clearly and concisely. State who you are, when you called and why; no intriguing mysteries, please. People who don't provide an explanation for their call often find it's left unreturned.

Mobile phones in the office. Ideally switch them off. A less satisfactory alternative: turn down the ring tone (particularly if it's of the novelty variety) and answer every call fast. Never leave your mobile phone at work when you've gone out – after it's rung for the third time, your colleagues are entitled to drop the thing into a sink of water.

YOUR COMPUTER
It's intended for work-related purposes only. Downloading porn from the internet on the office computer is inadvisable – there's a strong possibility you'll be found out (many companies have now installed software to detect the presence of porn), and as a result, quite legitimately, you'll be heavily penalized or even fired from your job. Lesser offences such as using your computer (and your work time) to write personal emails or even an 80,000 word novel are also liable to come to the attention of your superiors. They'll earn you, at the least, a reprimand. Save all non-work-related activities for your computer at home.

EMAILS
Because the medium's so immediate, it encourages spontaneity. But a few words of caution; what you think is spontaneous, somebody else might consider sloppy and unprofessional (with the threat of a correspondingly negative impact on your business). Rein in any desire to improvise, prepare drafts of whatever you're planning to send out into the ether, think about who else will see this and don't overlook the basics of punctuation and grammar – both can be speedily corrected on-screen.

Fellow Workers

PEOPLE SKILLS
Without question, any time spent at work will be easier and

more enjoyable if you're on good terms with your colleagues. Or, at the very least, if you can give that impression. The man sitting at the desk next to your own has an infuriating habit of noisily clearing his throat every few seconds (he also talks too loudly on the phone, has personal hygiene issues and is forever 'borrowing' your only pen). For the sake of a good working environment, try to keep any irritation to yourself – while requesting a transfer to another section of the building, of course. Part of the salary you're paid every month is actually for this purpose; to cover the cost of mental anguish caused by working with idiots. Likewise, you'll have to stifle the urge to contradict your boss when he gets his figures wrong, takes policy decisions you believe to be unwise or asks you to undertake a task you know will be detrimental to the company. They're your opinions, he has his. Harmony in the workplace advises that you keep yours to yourself. Or move somewhere else.

Time spent at work allows you to improve your people skills. It can be said with complete certainty that not getting along with the rest of the team won't improve things for you; in fact, it'll only make your circumstances worse. Don't want to get along with your colleagues? Have you considered the option of working from home?

All workplaces are divided into teams. Sometimes these divisions are obvious, sometimes they're not. Take the trouble to discover your own office teams and then make sure you're part of the winning side. This is called office politics and, like it or not, you ought to be a player. But play subtly; too obvious an allegiance can cause problems, especially if another team starts to show signs of winning. And keep an emotional distance from the game. Don't allow it to become a preoccupation. Understand that in organizations with a large workforce, some members of staff will do very little work because they're so immersed in office politics. Their days will be filled with covert meetings and discussions in which the latest twists and turns of internal struggles for power are analysed. You don't want to become one of these people because:

- They're only interested in the politics of the place, not its betterment.
- Their own careers have usually stalled and they're never going to advance further up the corporate ladder or leave the company currently employing them.

Be a contributor. Don't just do your own work and leave it at that. Offer something extra and there's every likelihood that you'll receive something extra in return – even if it's only a greater sense of personal satisfaction from a job well done.

Don't be too proud to ask for help, especially if the alternative's going to be that you make a mistake. How good for your career prospects would that be? So ask someone else if you're not sure how to address a superior, use the fax machine or find your way to the canteen.

In an open-plan office, keep your voice down, your perfume light and your opinions to yourself.

DEALING WITH RUDENESS

You're entitled to respond to bad behaviour with the remark, 'That's very rude.' Almost without fail, this proves astonishingly effective in silencing the offender.

Nevertheless, should the rudeness persist or start to interfere with your work, it might be necessary to take further action. Under these circumstances, you must make a formal complaint, either to your superior or, if one exists in your company, to the Human Resources department. When doing so, be specific rather than general. Your case won't be strengthened by broad-based or woolly accusations; keep a log of timed and dated incidents that can be presented as confirmation of your complaint.

Also prepare a strong argument demonstrating how these occasions of rudeness have adversely affected your work. Most companies have a poor record when it comes to dealing with issues of internal strife. The more clearly you show that acting on your complaint will be beneficial for the business, the sooner – and better – it will be dealt with.

BEING NICE
Whatever your initial place in the work hierarchy, you'll want to move upwards. That way, you earn more money, get better perks and might even be given a desk with a nice view out the window. On your climb up the professional ladder, remember to look behind as well as in front. Be every bit as nice to the people below you as above. None of us can ever be sure what changes in fortune will occur; the quiet girl who regularly offered to make you tea could suddenly become your boss (or start sleeping with him and therefore be just as influential). Did you forget to thank her every time she handed you a cup? Did you take her kindness for granted? The likelihood is that she'll now do the same thing to you. With every person you meet in the company, ask for a name and remember it, behave courteously, make introductions ('Jim, this is Madge, the cleaning lady. Madge, this is Jim, the managing director'), say good morning and good night. You don't have to become everyone's best friend; you do have to show courtesy.

LIFE AROUND THE WATER COOLER
Some people are irresistibly drawn there. In fact, they seem to spend more time fending off the risk of dehydration than they do at their desks. Between taking sips from a small paper cup, they'll be discussing everyone else at work. Office gossip – it's insidious and invidious and you don't want to be part of it. Start talking about your colleagues and it's only a matter of (a

little) time before they start talking about you.

Likewise, be careful about chatting on-line inside an office. The amusing message you sent to one colleague was then forwarded to another twenty – including the subject of your hilarity (who, for some reason, turns out to be much less amused than the rest of the office). There are now usually internal checks and guards on email and you can find yourself landed in serious trouble over what started out as a seemingly trivial joke about a secretary's thighs.

BECOMING BEST FRIENDS WITH A COLLEAGUE
Because you spend so much time together every week, it's inevitable that your social and professional lives are going to overlap. A note of caution about this. Firstly, it's healthy for you to have friends outside the work environment, if only to put the intensity of office politics into perspective. Not everyone, you'll soon discover, shares your preoccupation with the latest audacity of Janine on the switchboard. Other people talk about other things – like what was on television last night. You should do the same. Then there's the matter of changing circumstances: your best friend at work gets a promotion and you don't. Suddenly the two of you are operating on different levels. He's wearing a suit every day; you're still turning up in jeans. He's worried about meeting this month's sales figures; you're wondering what to have for lunch. He's spending Saturday afternoon at a management training seminar; you're spending it at a football match.

Unless you expect your circumstances at work never to change, don't depend on it entirely for your social life. If you, or one of your colleagues, is given promotion or simply a new position within the company, relations between you will alter – your roles have changed and so will your relationship.

SOCIALIZING WITH COLLEAGUES

Do so, but in moderation. How you behave with them outside the hours of work is going to affect how they perceive you inside the same. Don't offer any hostages to fortune; you go out for a drink with some workmates, the drink turns into several and by the end of the night you're slurring out your real opinion of the boss or how you lust after Christine in Telemarketing. That story will be told around work the following day and the way you're viewed will be adjusted accordingly. Without becoming a clam, remain cautious about speaking your mind on work-related topics to anyone in the same organization. In fact, keep all behaviour under control when in the company of colleagues. Fellow workers can have long memories and years after you want to forget the night you shimmied down the bar in full drag, they'll still be around to remind you – and one another – of the moment. And have the photographs to confirm their story.

Never drink at lunch unless it's a celebration thrown for your team by the company – and then keep consumption in moderation. If lunch is for wimps, drinking too much at lunchtime is for losers.

THE OFFICE ROMANCE

Your fellow workers will know about it. Oh no they won't? Oh yes they will. No matter how careful you both believe yourselves to have been, word about how/where/with whom you spent lunch hour in recent months will get about. It will then provide a fresh topic of conversation for regulars around the water cooler. That's fine if you're both single and without ties (in which case, there's no need for being careful). It's not so good if one or both of you are married/otherwise committed. It's also not good if there's a disparity between the two of you in the company hierarchy, i.e. one of you is the boss, the other's the

PA. In those circumstances, your personal life's apt to interfere with your work, whether you want/like it or not. And the interference almost certainly won't be to your advantage.

People will talk, and what do you care. That rather depends on what they're saying, doesn't it? Most probably they'll be saying that because you're now sleeping with the boss, his judgement about you is clouded and you're going to be given unfair privileges at work.

Another reason why the office romance carries risks: it mightn't last. You'll then have the problem of sharing a workplace with your former lover. If the break-up was in any way acrimonious, the consequences could affect your job, your performance, possibly even your future prospects in the company. Avoid these risks by keeping your love life away from work.

SEX WITH A COLLEAGUE
Quite different from an office romance – or is it? Are you sure both of you feel the same way; that it was just an amusing conclusion to this year's Christmas party? Sex on the desk with a fellow worker seems wonderful at the time but there's always a morning of reckoning. Are you prepared for reproachful stares across the photocopier? Or for an outbreak of tittering every time you walk past the coffee dock? Overall, it's probably wiser not to mix sex and business at all.

DISPLAYS OF SEXISM
And any other forms of negative discrimination at work – based on age, gender, sexual inclination, race. Mostly they're proscribed by law but all of us can be guilty of them, often without realizing it at the time. What you considered a casual remark, trivial action or amusing story might have been perceived by one of your colleagues as a calculated effort to undermine his/her position. Maybe you think people should be tougher,

better able to take a joke and less inclined to find offence in what – to your mind – is obviously something trivial. However, this attitude won't serve as a good defence when you're summoned before an Industrial Relations Tribunal. Take the sensibilities of other workers into account before you speak or act.

HOW TO BEHAVE WELL AT A MEETING (AND STILL GET WHAT YOU WANT)

- ✦ Make your presence felt, without being too dominant. This means contributing to the discussion but not trying to control it.
- ✦ Encourage the other participants to speak before you. This'll give you time to prepare your own contribution while becoming aware of their ideas and proposals – and seeing the merits/drawbacks of these.
- ✦ State your case clearly, attributing at least some of its advantages to people who spoke earlier ('As Jim so cleverly pointed out just now ...'). This tactic has the effect of drawing them onto your side. Seek to achieve consensus as much as possible. Pay particular attention to whoever's trying to become the meeting's alpha male (it could be a woman). Make sure that you have him or her in broad agreement with you, otherwise you'll become bogged in a tedious, time-consuming and unnecessary power struggle. Yes, you want to win – it's just that sometimes you can't be seen to win.
- ✦ Allow for compromise. Concede on lesser details and you're much more likely to be successful in your principal argument. Battle to get your own way on every minor point and you could lose the major one.
- ✦ Don't feel the need to have it publicly acknowledged that you got what you wanted. Your victory was probably someone else's defeat. By drawing attention to yourself, you run

the risk of making enemies. And at the next meeting, they'll be even more determined to stop you getting your own way.

Working with People Outside the Office

Always return phone calls. As soon as possible. Firstly, this is just basic courtesy. Secondly, it will make you appear dynamic and professional (even if, in fact, you're a slovenly amateur). Thirdly, the person who rang you will appreciate this display of good manners and, most likely, show similar consideration in any subsequent dealings with you. And fourthly, if you don't deal with all calls promptly, they've a nasty habit of building up until they become an intimidating mountain.

Likewise with letters and emails. Set aside enough time to deal with these every day. By attending to your correspondence daily, you'll find not much time is actually needed. Never say you're too busy to do this; it's sloppy and unprofessional and won't help you succeed.

Turn up for meetings on time. Being late and/or keeping other people waiting is inadvisable. It puts you at a strategic disadvantage and it puts them in a bad mood. You're representing the company, do so to the best of your abilities. At the meeting, be thoroughly professional, make sure you're well-briefed, have all relevant documentation with you (or commit yourself to getting it to the other party as soon as possible), switch off your mobile phone and switch on your charm. Remember that reports on how you've behaved inside work hours but outside the usual work environment will, somehow, filter back to your boss at HQ.

The Boss

BE ON GOOD TERMS

You and your boss don't have to be best friends; you do have to be able to work well together. This'll be harder in a hostile environment. And because you're not the boss, you're more likely to suffer the consequences of any hostility. So, much as you might dislike or despise or deride the boss, keep all such feelings to yourself.

Bad blood between yourself and the boss? Sort it out quickly. This'll probably mean a certain amount of humble pie consumption on your part but better to cut yourself a slice now than be obliged to eat the entire thing later. In a dispute between the boss and an underling, the latter has to lose because otherwise the former's authority is called into question. Don't take losing too much to heart – it's only work, after all, and not the Third World War.

However, if you feel the dispute/difference of opinion is over a really fundamental matter of principle and that you can't back down or apologize gracefully, now's the time to start looking at the situations vacant columns in the national media.

On the other hand, if you find yourself regularly coming into conflict with the boss, the problem's probably not one of principle but of temperament – either that of your employer or of you. Ask yourself whether you're suited to work in a hierarchical environment and be answerable to people further up the corporate ladder. Not everyone's a team player or prepared to take direction from a manager. You can't change your character, you can change your circumstances. Look into the possibilities of working for yourself where there'll be only one person to whom you're answerable: you.

DISCREET SCHMOOZING

Overt efforts to draw attention to yourself won't win plaudits from your colleagues. The boss needs to discover your merits as though by accident rather than by any obvious design. And this will happen quite naturally if you're good at your job. Only inadequate professionals have to seek out attention.

Be duly grateful for any help given to you by the boss. Don't take it for granted, say thank you. That's not being sycophantic, it's being polite.

ASKING FOR A RISE

Or a change of position within the company? Hoping to be given a vacant desk by the window? Ask and you shall receive, provided that your request is made in the right way. As in any other circumstance where you can't be certain of getting what you want, preparation is essential. Plan what you want to say, think of good arguments in support of your case and also ask yourself what counter-arguments could be produced. Then prepare responses to these. Forewarned is forearmed: you're much more likely to have your salary increased if you present a strong argument in support of this rather than merely saying you'd like more money. Rehearse your pitch with someone who can play devil's advocate, that way you'll do a better job when it comes to the real thing. And don't be despondent should your request be turned down. Ambition and drive (even if it's only manifested in the longing for a window view) will never be frowned upon. By asking for more, evidence has been given of your sense of self-worth. Just make sure your work record confirms this view.

PARTYING WITH THE BOSS

As a rule, it's better not to do so. Anxiety about presenting yourself in the best possible light before your boss while socializing with him/her can cause you to act in a slightly/somewhat/completely ridiculous manner. If you become friendly with your boss for a time and then the two of you have a disagreement, the effects of this could spill over into the work environment. Whenever possible, turn down invitations from your boss while making it clear that you're suitably grateful they've been made.

Sometimes, though, you won't be given the choice of refusal. There are times when saying no might damage your career, while saying yes could advance it. On these occasions, of course, the latter's your only option, so make play outside the office work to your advantage.

Firstly, try not to be nervous or excessively anxious about making a good impression. Don't make a commitment to do anything outside your usual range of abilities. Your boss invites you to spend the afternoon on the local golf course and you've never played the game? This isn't an opportune moment to make your début. Apologize and, if you know anything about your boss's other interests, suggest an alternative engagement that would suit you both.

Be yourself. Present your boss with much the same person already known from the office. Avoid drinking too much or being too obsequious. Don't defer excessively and don't be afraid to assert opinions as you would on any other social occasion. You've made a total fool of yourself? Apologize immediately and sincerely; if your boss is even half-decent, this ought to be enough to allow the incident be forgotten once you're both back in the workplace.

Take your lead from your boss without appearing too sycophantic. If he's the one proposing midnight skinny-dipping, then it's okay for you to join in. But if he turns up poolside wearing a dressing gown and an expression of disapproval, you can take it that throwing aside your reticence and your clothes was an unwise career move. Apologize fast if you become conscious of overstepping that invisible boundary in either speech or behaviour. Then pray this won't affect your next salary review. And just because it's a work-related event, you're not excused from showing appreciation for any hospitality received. Writing a letter to the boss afterwards is going too far; saying thanks isn't.

When Work Doesn't Work

Be wary of staying in any job that leaves you feeling dissatisfied. You won't give it your best and it won't bring out the best in you. In that scenario, no one's a winner. Feeling discontented? Weigh up the checks and balances. You could resist moving jobs for any or all of the following reasons:

- Fear of the unknown, especially if you've been doing the same work for more than five years.
- Fear that nobody else will ever offer you alternative employment.
- Fear of a sudden drop in your income (and you haven't put aside any savings for this eventuality).

All of these concerns are valid but none of them should stop you leaving your present job, especially if you're not enjoying it. Fear ought to be a spur to change, not a hindrance. Get a sheet of paper and write out two lists, one covering your financial outgoings and assets, the other looking at your qualifications and aspirations in the job market. Then draw up a plan for yourself for the year ahead with specific, and realistically achievable, goals. In the short-term, your income will probably dip but most of us can easily find ways of cutting back our expenditure such as shopping more sensibly, taking fewer holidays or temporarily getting rid of the car. Ask around: you'll discover that people who've changed jobs rarely, if ever, say they regret leaving their old position. More usually, they say their only regret was not leaving it sooner. Hanging onto a job for the sake of your retirement pension is never going to make you happy.

9. Modern Communication

Takes an enormous variety of different forms. Learn some elementary skills for each of them and you'll find making contact with the world around you much easier.

A note of caution: Almost every form of communication can, and most likely will, be saved in some form or another by the recipient. Letters, emails, text messages: potentially they have a life long after leaving you. Usually that's fine, but there are occasions – especially anything sent in a blur of anger – when the wiser course is to remain incommunicado.

Letters

Despite all the alternatives now available to us, they're still a wonderful method of communication.

Why? Because a letter will always let its lucky recipient know that you've taken trouble and made an extra effort to get in touch. Letters are obviously more time-consuming and harder work than sending a 'Lvly 2 C U' text message. They're more permanent than a phone call. And they're more tangible than an email. Their other advantage is rarity: the majority of us now only receive dreary bills and junk mail in the morning's post. A personal letter immediately stands out as something special.

Feel you lack the necessary writing skills? Don't worry, so few people write letters of any kind today that even the humblest effort will win you kudos. Avoid flowery prose, state what you need to say plainly and you'll do just fine. As with the spoken word, getting to the point clearly and speedily never fails to be appreciated. Working on the principle that practice makes perfect, one way to improve your letter-writing technique is to get into the habit of doing it. Then, even if perfection still eludes you, at least your letters will show the benefit of plenty of experience.

There's no shame in admitting you've trouble coming up with the right words. Better to do that than not writing at all and leaving your friend with a belief that you just couldn't be bothered to get in touch at a time of need.

Concerned about your spelling and grammar? Invest in a pocket dictionary, along with a simple guide to writing well such as *Fowler's Modern English Usage* or Lynne Truss's *Eats, Shoots & Leaves*. Use these particularly when you're uncertain about something in your letter.

It's useful to set aside a specific time every week for dealing with all your correspondence, perhaps Monday evening or any other slot in your calendar which you know is likely to be quiet. Use this period not only to take care of household bills and the like but also your personal letters, the ones thanking hosts for their hospitality or making contact with family members who live overseas.

THANK YOU LETTERS
Still doubtful of the ability to express yourself well? Whether you want to say 'I love you', 'thank you' or 'get well soon', it's fine

to buy a card more articulate than you are and just add your signature.

Your letter doesn't have to be much but it does have to be legible. Why send someone a letter that can't be read? Copperplate script isn't required but do write in block letters if there's a risk your scribblings will be undecipherable.

The appearance of your letter is as important as its contents. If you don't have your own printed stationery – and the majority of people don't – keep a stock of attractive cards you can use for this purpose. But do make sure they have their own envelopes; there's something so much more personal about getting a sealed letter rather than an open postcard, the details of which can be read by anyone. When travelling abroad, track down smart box-sets of cards in museums and art galleries for this purpose. And try to match the image shown on the card with the person to whom you're writing. A busty girl on a beach for your grandmother? Probably not. It's this kind of thoughtful detail that makes all the difference.

WHEN A LETTER IS THE BEST FORM OF COMMUNICATION

- To commiserate with someone in a time of trouble (family bereavement, bad health, loss of job, etc.).
- To say thank you (for a present, a meal, an act of kindness).
- To make a formal complaint. Take your time, never write in the first flush of anger, state your case plainly and you're far more likely to get a response that'll be to your satisfaction. (*Tip:* Write the letter and then put it away for twenty-four hours, read over what you've written again and, if you're still happy, then send it.)
- To say you're sorry. Don't worry too much about how you say this; the act of your writing is sufficiently symbolic.

NEVER WRITE A LETTER WHEN
- You're angry.
- You're drunk.
- You're both of the above.

Fax

Although not that old, the fax has been almost entirely super-seded by further technological advances like email. Even so, it has certain uses, primarily as a means of sending facsimile copies of documents from one person to another. Today the fax is most likely to be a business device but that doesn't mean you can jettison good manners.

Always send a cover sheet with whatever material you're fax-ing. On this, you should write your own name, address, tele-phone and fax number together with the name of the intended recipient. Then if you've sent it to the wrong place (it happens), the person who unwittingly received your fax can let you know what's happened. Also write on the cover sheet how many pages can be expected – this last detail is terribly helpful to the other party who otherwise mightn't realize only half of your commu-nication has come through.

Because they're printed out immediately, faxes aren't the best way to send private, confidential or contentious material, espe-cially since the fax machine at the other end is probably in a public office. Check with the recipient first if you're worried about anyone else seeing what you plan to send. Alternatively, be prepared for your marital troubles to become common knowl-edge.

Keep it short – the fax machine shouldn't have to spit out dozens of pages. If you've a lot of material to send, do so by email attachment.

As the fax is really a business tool, don't use it for sending either invitations or thank yous. There are many more personal ways of doing both.

Email

Is excellent for both your professional and personal life. But do distinguish between the two. In a work context, the tone of your emails ought to be less jocular and more formal than would otherwise be the case. Because the medium is so instant, it encourages casualness among users. Beware of allowing this to happen to your business emails; the people reading them could imagine you're not serious about your work and react to you accordingly.

The great majority of internet service providers offer their users a free email address. This means you can have one for your professional life and one for your personal life (as well as one for the side of your personality that likes to be tied up and lightly spanked with a hairbrush). By keeping them separate, you'll find it easier to compartmentalize your business email correspondence.

If the medium does lead you to adopt a relaxed, conversational tone, really serious business shouldn't be conducted by email. In these circumstances, a letter is preferable.

Especially in the workplace, beware of the temptation to send 'jokey' emails. Not everyone will share the same sense of humour. Your supposedly funny office email will quickly pass between other members of staff until it reaches someone who isn't amused – usually your boss. And yes, legally emails can be deemed libellous.

You're a regular email user with a wide circle of people who keep in touch by this means? Whenever you're going to be incommunicado for any period longer than a couple of days, leave a message explaining your temporary absence – it can be sent automatically to anyone who emails during this time and will explain why there's no response from you.

Everyone who has an email address is entitled to keep this private. Don't send around a group email that carries the addresses of all your other correspondents.

Chain emails – of the kind that promise if you pass on the enclosed message to another ten people you'll unexpectedly win the lottery or find romantic fulfilment – are infantile and annoying. Attached, there's usually also a dire warning about what will happen if you don't forward the message, with examples of the bad luck experienced by someone who foolishly ignored this advice. If you get one, unless you want to look completely gullible, don't forward it to your friends. Delete the message at once and tell whoever sent it that in future you'd rather not receive any more.

Speed is one of the greatest advantages of email. It's also one of its greatest hazards. If you write an email when angry or upset, let it sit overnight. Your mood could have changed by the following morning.

Delete all spam emails immediately and without opening them. If you read your spam emails, the person who sent them (one old lady running a highly profitable porn business from her living-room in Utah) will presume you're interested and continue to bombard you with offers of discounted Viagra, penis enlargement and lesbian sex.

Telephone

Talking on the telephone is just like any other conversation, except that you can't see the other person. For the moment anyway, although this could soon change.

At the start of the call, if there's even the slightest chance that the person at the other end of the line won't recognize your voice, state your name. There's almost nothing more irritating than a call from an apparent stranger beginning, 'Hi, how are you?' The only response to this is, 'Who are you?' Never take it for granted that everyone knows who you are – remember, they can't see you.

Just because you can't see the person on the other end of the line, permission hasn't been given for you to share your attention. Turn off the television, put down the magazine, quit surfing the internet. Or, if you really can't stop whatever it is you're doing at that moment, explain this to the caller and ask if you could call back later. Then make sure you do so. Likewise, if you're eating or drinking at the time of the call, please say so; it's no fun chatting to someone whose mouth is full of food.

It's a good idea to ask the person you've rung if this is a convenient time to talk. The answer's no? Offer to ring again and find out when would be best.

Particularly if you think the person on the other end of the line has other business requiring immediate attention, don't linger on the phone. Want to talk further? End the call by arranging to meet at a mutually convenient time.

ANSWERING MACHINES/VOICEMAIL

They're no longer a novelty, we all have them, so there's really no need to leave a message on yours informing callers that they're speaking to a machine, not a person. Do give your name or some other indication that the caller has rung the intended number. Reply to any messages, otherwise the caller will assume you didn't get it. Check your messages regularly. Even when you're away from home, it's still possible check them. If you don't do this, your mailbox will fill up and later callers mightn't be able to leave you a message.

Remember to keep it short and speak clearly, don't garble

and leave your name ('It's me,' is never a helpful opening line) as well as the date and time of your call and, finally, your telephone number. Say the last of these slowly and then repeat it – numbers are often incorrectly written down because they're given too fast or indistinctly. After doing all that, hang up.

MOBILE PHONES

Incredibly convenient and incredibly annoying. Somehow we all managed perfectly well before they came along, but then again, our ancestors survived without electricity, running water, decent sewerage disposal and the addition of 2 per cent Lycra to stretch denim – and who wants to return to those days? Mobile phones are not going away, they're a permanent feature of contemporary life. Get used to them.

That said, there are considerate and inconsiderate mobile phone users and almost nothing is more annoying than a member of the latter group. Your mobile phone should be taken from you and trampled underfoot if:

- You always feel the necessity to talk VERY LOUDLY whenever using it.
- You let it ring on and on in a public place.
- You have a so-called personal ring tone that is supposedly based, tangentially, on Queen's 'Bohemian Rhapsody'. And you let this ring on and on in a public place.
- You take a call while out with other people (and so let them know how important you imagine yourself to be).
- You take out your phone at business meetings and place it on the table in front of you. (What? You think nobody else in the room has got one?)
- You walk along the street talking into a hands-free phone and thereby give the impression of being mildly deranged.
- You send text messages when in the company of other people. And then give a private little smile while reading the reply.

THINK OF OTHERS

Mobile phone use demands consideration. No one wants to eavesdrop on your conversations or hear the obvious stated. 'I'm on the bus.' Guess what: so are all the passengers around you, but they don't feel the need to tell this to anyone else. Other people will not appreciate your ring tone, particularly if it's loud and isn't switched off quickly. Other people will not relish having lunch or a business meeting interrupted by a mobile phone call, no matter how urgent you claim it to be. And people will decide you're just plain rude if you begin texting when with them.

Use a mobile phone for whatever purpose you like while on your own. Otherwise, first think of how other people will judge your rudeness.

TEXTING

Is generally cheaper than talking on your mobile phone. It's also useful for quick messages such as asking someone you're sup-

Darling! – They're playing our ring tone

posed to meet, 'Where are you?' Notice that those three words have been spelt fully and correctly. Text abbreviation is fine for teenagers but after that it can look a bit sad, the equivalent of someone middle-aged trying to act hip by saying things like 'chill out' or announcing that rap is today's equivalent of Wordsworth's sonnets. As with skateboarding and illicit smoking behind the bicycle shed, the language of text abbreviation belongs to the young. Bear in mind too that not everybody will be as fluent in text-speak as U R.

Keep your text exchanges short – they're no substitute for a proper conversation.

Don't text when you're with other people.

SENDING PICTURES ON YOUR MOBILE PHONE
Wonderful in theory, slightly questionable in practice as a few well-publicized instances in the media have shown. Send a picture of a beautiful landscape, that's fine. But send a picture of someone else to a third party and questions about invasion of privacy start to be asked. What if the person whose photograph you've sent to friends was supposed to be somewhere else or with someone else at the time? Did you ask permission before taking the picture and putting it into the public domain? What will subsequently happen to a picture of your best friend prancing around in her underwear (or even less clothing)? It could be further distributed by mobile phone, appear on an internet website, be published in a magazine. The consequences of mobile phone photography have yet to be fully appreciated. Before taking and sending a picture by this method, understand that you could be infringing another individual's rights.

10. Flat Living: How to Survive Other People

When you're living in a cheek-by-jowl scenario with people you know barely or not at all, courtesy and consideration are incredibly important. So too is understanding the basic tenets of communal life, the first of which is that not everyone else in the building thinks or behaves in the same way as you.

Neighbours

Antagonism between neighbours living in the same building is likely to occur because of the following circumstances:

- ✤ Most modern developments have thin walls and insufficient sound insulation between adjoining homes. Sound will travel, especially at night and especially if music and/or conversation is loud. Keeping down both during the wee small hours greatly reduces the likelihood of friction between neighbours.
- ✤ Some residents have a poor appreciation of security and won't properly close the main doors into the apartment

complex. As a result, non-residents – some of them with criminal intent – will be able to gain admission to the building. The next time there's a burglary in the building, you could be the victim.

- ✤ Residents don't always understand the dual advantages of maintaining the complex's public areas. The first is simply a matter of aesthetics: the place looks better if it's kept well. But there's also a powerful financial incentive too: if you allow the hallway and corridors to grow shabby, they'll have to be regularly repaired and repainted – and that, in turn, will cost money. Not so complicated really, is it?

All apartments within a complex come with an annual service fee that goes towards paying communal obligations such as insurance and waste collection as well as a fee for the company hired to take care of the building's management. But the complex will also have its own residents' committee. If you're interested in the welfare of the place (and you ought to be, considering the price paid for your apartment) it's worth becoming an active member of this. That way, you can make sure the building is well maintained and that problems are kept to a minimum. The more active the residents' committee, the better run the complex. Joining the committee is also an excellent way of getting to know some of your fellow residents because apartment living can be quite solitary.

Tenants and Landlords

These two groups often tend to behave as though they're engaged in a form of ongoing guerrilla warfare against one another. It usually starts with covert acts of terrorism like the mysterious kidnapping of a teapot lid and gradually escalates to open hostilities of the kind that need a United Nations Peacekeeping Force to resolve. Experience has shown that nobody can hope to emerge as winner from this kind of scenario, and nobody's particularly happy with it either. Just ask someone who's ever been either a landlord or a tenant (but set aside a couple of hours to hear the succession of horror stories). Remember also that disputes between tenants and landlords are among the most frequent cases to come before the small claims courts.

The best way to avoid potential conflict is for both parties to consider the other not as an enemy but an ally. This means each must observe the following rules of engagement:

TENANTS
- No matter how badly neglected the property you're renting, it's still not your right to make it even worse. Keep the place at least up to the standard in which you found it (even if that standard wasn't high in the first place).
- If you've a problem with anything on the premises, announce this as soon as possible (the more time you allow to elapse, the more likely the landlord will claim the problem's arisen only since you became the tenant). Try to state your case in a pleasant manner. And be persistent; many landlords can suffer lapses of memory when it comes to looking after the requirements of their tenants.
- If you damage or break anything included in the rental, replace it at once – and tell your landlord that you've done so.
- Remember that you have legal rights and are entitled to exercise these, although with a difficult landlord, that could entail finding somewhere else to live. But wouldn't this be preferable to staying in a hostile atmosphere?

LANDLORDS
- Your tenants are more likely to respect the property you're

renting if it's reasonably maintained and furnished. If you don't show any concern for the state of the place, why should they?

- ☛ Respect your tenants' privacy. This means not entering the premises whenever it suits you (which, by the way, isn't legally permitted). If you, or your agent, are collecting rent on a weekly basis, arrange that this be done at a mutually agreeable time.
- ☛ By law, you're obliged to give your tenant a rental book. This will also make it much easier for both of you to monitor what money is due, and when.
- ☛ The initial deposit paid when the rental contract is signed shouldn't be seen as an extra donation to your bank account. It's a down-payment that has to be returned when the tenant quits the property.

Flat-Sharing

This is a form of performance art. Of the kind that leads the rest of us to say, 'I could do that, no problem,' until we're asked to. Suddenly it proves to be a lot more challenging than it seemed. In fact, living with other people is difficult (just ask any married couple you know). This is because all members of the human race are territorial; it's part of our genetic make-up, like having two eyes or flexible thumbs. Marking our own territory while sharing a flat or house poses challenges but it will nevertheless be attempted, whether through claiming rights to a specific corner of the fridge or by leaving beer cans scattered across the living-room floor. Both these acts, along with many others, are intended to send out a clear signal that a particular terrain has been marked as belonging to us alone. Except, of course, that it doesn't because the other residents of the house/flat will also want to use the fridge and living-room. And they're entitled to do so.

What's the best way to avoid rows when living with other people? Resist the temptation to mark out your own territory in the communal rooms. It's really that simple. If you've a burning desire to give expression to your own unique personality, do so within the confines of your bedroom.

KEEP IT CLEAN

As a rule, men are worse than women at taking care of household chores. One reason is that as children they were not expected to do so. (All mothers responsible for producing these offspring, hang your heads in shame.) They think alpha males shouldn't be responsible for looking after themselves. This is true even of men who could never be considered alpha male material. Although now adults, when left on their own for any length of time, men quickly revert to a state of helpless infantilism. They believe that somewhere there exists a woman who'll be prepared to take care of both them and all of the chores.

Women are generally more house-proud than men and possess a better understanding of the merits of cleanliness. However, even this is an acquired skill. Teenage girls, for example, often display a touching belief that the bedroom floor is a better place to store their clothes than the wardrobe.

How to keep the place clean? Establish a rota of duties between residents or, if this seems too much like returning to school, come to an agreement about who'll be responsible for which tasks. Learn one of the great secrets of good housekeeping: the more regularly you clean something, the less time it takes to do so.

All of you should look after certain obvious duties, such as:

- Washing your own dishes after you've eaten.
- Rinsing your own hairs out of the bath.

- Putting your own CDs back into their cases.

If you don't do this, soon the outcome will be stalemate, with all of you refusing to wash a plate and none of you having anything clean to eat from. An unhealthy diet of finger food follows, accompanied by efforts to cook packet soup in the kettle.

None of you want to clean the place? Pay somebody to do so once a week. When divided between all the residents, the price per person shouldn't be too high (not much more than the cost of a pint or two). It will be money well spent.

FRIENDS AND LOVERS

You'll want to entertain your friends in the flat. Do so only after informing other residents of your plans. One flatmate might come home planning a quiet night in front of the television and find twenty people packed into the kitchen and a queue outside the bathroom. This is not a good way to keep internal relations sweet.

Friends who drop in without warning should be welcomed, but also told if there's someone in the flat who's gone to bed early/not feeling well/anti-social. Otherwise the night could end with an ugly confrontation.

Food and drink belonging to other residents are off-limits to your friends, even if there's nothing else on the premises. Discover the telephone numbers of your local off-licence and takeaway. A subsequent promise to replace the missing six-pack of beer won't make up for its initial disappearance. Likewise, if your friends play another flatmate's CDs, at least leave them tidy afterwards.

Occasionally you'll want to entertain someone who's more than a friend. The sight of a stranger emerging from the bathroom the following morning will provide endless opportunities for amusement and gossip among your flatmates. As a result, they won't mind the presence of another person on the premises. Provided, of course, that the presence is temporary. If you're bringing the same someone back to a shared flat night after night, it's good manners and good sense to check with the other residents that they've no objections to this arrangement. They agreed to share a place with you, not with you and your girl/boyfriend. Failure to discuss this could lead to friction, particularly if your flatmates don't like said girl/boyfriend. Also, another person in the apartment puts additional strain on communal resources. Should the boy/girlfriend become a regular on the premises, it's a good idea that he/she offer to make a contribution to the rent. That'll certainly make his/her presence more palatable.

Unless you're an exhibitionist, it's wisest in a flatshare to save all expressions of your affection for somebody else until the two of you are alone in your bedroom. One of the other residents will, without fail, amble into the living-room just as you're engaged in a complicated manoeuvre involving the removal of a bra. This is not the best moment for social introductions. Save those for when you're all fully dressed.

To repeat a point made earlier: flat walls are poorly soundproofed. The flat's other residents will hear whatever athletic activity takes place in your bedroom, whether they want to or not. But how much or how little they hear is your choice. Expect comments on your performance to be passed the following day. What you got up to will be judged poorly but these comments, you can be sure, have been inspired by nothing more than envy.

PARTIES
It's an axiom of flat living that you're going to host parties regularly. These events are more likely to be successful if:

- You first check that your flatmates are happy with the idea of a party. The alternative is that they'll walk into the place and discover their bed covered in coats on top of which lie two people who only met an hour earlier but are now in the process of getting to know each other much better.
- You encourage your flatmates to invite some of their own friends. That way, you'll also get to meet some new people.
- You persuade all flatmates who're staying on the premises for your party to contribute to its costs in proportion to the number of friends they invite. If 50 per cent of the guests are theirs, so is 50 per cent of the night's expenditure.
- You ask all guests to bring a bottle. Some of them won't, that's just the way it is.
- You notify the residents of other flats or houses in the vicinity that you're holding a party. It's better they find out this way rather than the alternative: being woken up by a racket

I insist you join us — We adore new people!

at three in the morning. You might like to invite the neighbours to come along. They probably won't do so, but they also probably won't ring the police to complain about the noise your guests are making.

~ You pay attention when a neighbour does complain – either in person or via the police. Remember, you still have to live next to these people long after your party's become a distant memory. Complaints will always be about noise: lower it. Your guests still won't be quiet? Take the party somewhere else (a bar/a club/the house of a friend who doesn't have any neighbours).

~ You prepare yourself for the fact that the morning after the night before both the kitchen and bathroom are going to be in a condition of previously unimaginable squalor. Anticipating a mess won't make the squalor (or your hangover) any less appalling but at least it won't come as a total shock.

~ You accept, as party host, that you're responsible for cleaning up afterwards. If all the flatmates threw the party together, all of you are responsible. That's the deal.

~ You expect that something will be broken, from the television set to your heart. No party can be called a success unless there are casualties. This doesn't mean you need to end the night spending several hours in the nearest hospital's Accident and Emergency department.

~ You're ready if guests start behaving badly. Get them off the premises fast; you don't want to be responsible for any trouble in your home.

~ You appreciate as an inevitability that a handful of guests at your party will be strangers; they're the gate-crashers. Unless you see them pocketing your CDs or dealing drugs, let them stay. Turfing out harmless gate-crashers can be hard work and will create a bad atmosphere at the party.

INTERNAL COMMUNICATIONS

Flatmates row, usually about the most trivial matters: who used the last of the milk; who emptied the hot-water tank for a bath; whose box of junk has been sitting in the hall for the past three weeks.

At least one of you won't stick to the agreed house rules. Someone in the flat will be forever eating your food last thing at night (but will insist on describing this petty act of theft as 'borrowing') or will forget to hoover the living-room – every week. You can try to enforce house rules but it won't be easy and it probably won't be successful. What you'll never manage to do is change your flatmates' temperaments. If the differences turn out to be irreconcilable, find somewhere else to live.

As any marriage counsellor can confirm, the best way to avoid rows is through regular communication with each other. Communication can take place via a number of ways, probably the least helpful of which is leaving angry notes attached to the fridge door with a Mr Smiley magnet. If you've something to say to one of your flatmates, say it but only speak your mind when your mind's calm. Angry speeches will antagonize the other person and won't help your cause.

Choose the right moment for communication: not in the middle of a soccer final on television or at eight in the morning when everyone's dashing out of the flat.

When you do speak, point out whatever you believe to be the problem and leave it at that. Don't look for apologies or evidence of contrition or promises that whatever's annoyed you will never happen again. Because, unfortunately, it will.

FOOD AND THE KITCHEN

The kitchen must be kept reasonably clean, otherwise bacteria will breed and someone will catch something gastric and nasty. The cooker, fridge, sink and work surfaces should be cleaned thoroughly and regularly. This is common sense and will reduce the chances of food poisoning.

From the start, agree among yourselves either to pool money for food into a communal kitty or each to buy your own. Both arrangements have advantages and drawbacks. With a communal kitty, there can be no arguments about who's eating whose food because all of it belongs to all of you. On the other hand, someone will have to be in charge of shopping for groceries and you mightn't like whatever's being bought. Or the designated person could forget to go shopping and then you mightn't like the fact that there's nothing to eat. With pooling all the food in the place, there's also the potential problem of certain flatmates eating more than others, or your arriving home in the evening to discover what had been a full packet of biscuits that morning is now empty.

The merits of each flatmate taking responsibility for his/her own food shopping are obvious; you've got what you want, when you want it. That's the theory; the practice will be a bit different. In a shared flat, food has a way of wandering away from your shelf onto someone else's. Unless you're planning to put a lock on your cupboard, another flatmate will drink some of your coffee (topped up with a splash of your milk).

It's probably best to agree a communal monthly fund for certain basic household groceries (bread, butter, etc.) and then make each resident assume personal responsibility for the rest. But never expect your milk to be safe from poaching.

THE BATHROOM
Unless you're in a posh flat and have your own bathroom, get used to spending some time there, but not all the time. Other people like to wash too, particularly during the morning rush hour. Experienced flatsharers already appreciate the advantage of pre-allotted time slots for the morning sessions in the bath-

room. That way each of you will know precisely when you can be sure the place is yours.

Night time bathroom use can be more leisurely. Even so, someone else will eventually want to get in there; don't lock yourself away for hours. Heating water can be an expensive business and this'll be reflected in your electricity bills. If you like to have a lot of full baths, be prepared to pay for your extravagance. Showers are much more economical (and faster).

As with the kitchen, each of you will have your own bathroom belongings. Ideally, there ought to be a shelf allotted per resident. Resist the temptation to try out your flatmate's anti-perspirant/perfume/make-up/shaving blade. If you're worried about other people pinching your dental floss, keep it in your bedroom in a washbag.

A good rule to follow is that you should try to leave the bathroom as you'd like to find it. No one is going to appreciate a legacy of your hairs in the shower, whether these came from your head or elsewhere.

Have your own towel and keep it in your bedroom – spread out so that it can dry and be aired. Don't leave your towel in the bathroom: it offers a temptation more powerful than chocolate and will definitely be used by your flatmates. *Note:* towels are unable to dry themselves when left lying on the bathroom floor.

PRIVACY
Is the hardest thing to find in a shared flat. If you're a naturally private person, expect to find yourself severely tested. Finances permitting, it might be better for you to rent by yourself. Finances not permitting, prepare to spend a lot of time in your own room.

If you're a gregarious character and you share a flat, understand that the other residents mightn't be as sociable. Show consideration and do the greater amount of your partying off-site.

This will make relations with more reticent flatmates far easier.

Each flatmate's bedroom is sacrosanct. Imagine a large notice on the door saying 'Do Not Enter' and follow this instruction unless invited to do otherwise. Don't imagine yourself free to wander in and out of other people's rooms.

Borrowing your flatmate's belongings: only if you've asked first and been told that it's alright. Never presume permission.

MONEY

Will cause arguments. It always does.

Communal bills (electricity/gas/telephone) should be split evenly between flatmates. This is much simpler than trying to work out fractions of use by arguing that one of you spends more time on the phone than the others. But if somebody is adding disproportionately to the household bills, whether by taking a bath every night or talking for two hours to his girl-friend in Australia, this needs to be discussed by all of you and an arrangement on costs agreed. Have the conversation as soon as possible, preferably even before the bill arrives.

When you first move into a flat, ask either the landlord or the other residents about the approximate monthly costs. This'll make your budgeting easier.

You must pay your share of a bill when requested to do so. Asking your flatmates to carry you financially will lead to bad feelings and could cause a rift between you all. Borrow from the bank, not your friends. If you pay back the debt late, the bank will penalize you but it won't slam the door and say it's never going to speak to you again.

Most basic service providers provide an itemized bill if asked to do so. This will help you to break down costs and see where the greatest and least amount of money is being spent. It will also reduce the likelihood of any argument among flat-mates.

Remember that staying on the internet for a long time can be expensive.

Payment of bills. One of you will have to collect the money from the others and send it to the electricity or telephone company. Do so within the permitted time; it's no fun to come home on a winter night and discover that, thanks to a flatmate's temporary amnesia, the electricity supply has been cut off. Cue another argument.

11. Diverse Social Interaction

In theory, driving manners couldn't be simpler – just look over the *Rules of the Road*. Unless, of course, you've recently passed your driving test. In which case, the first thing you did after leaving the test centre was to bin your meticulously annotated copy of the *Rules of the Road*. Should this be the case, acquire another copy to keep in the car. Even if you never read the text again, its margins will be invaluable for writing directions to other people's houses on.

Driving Manners

SPEED

There is a direct correlation between a driver's sense of self-importance and the speed at which he is travelling. The faster you drive, the more important you imagine yourself to be. Fast drivers like to believe themselves critical to a nation's well-being. However, the fact that the sandwiches resting on your passenger seat are required immediately in an office on the other side of the city will not be thought an adequate excuse for breaking the speed limit, particularly by the law and its enforcers. The latter are responsible for creating another correlation; that between drivers caught speeding and a subsequent endorsement of their licences (as well as an increase in their insurance premiums). Don't like the laws on speeding? Consider standing for election as a public representative and then you can change them. Otherwise, your ideal correlation is between the prescribed speed limit and a clean licence. One other point: speed limits are usually set for a specific purpose – and that is to ensure that you, and anyone in your vicinity at the time, live long enough to continue using the road.

If the driver in front is proceeding at 10 miles per hour in a 30-mile area, curb the temptation to indicate irritation by flashing your lights or sounding your horn. Slow drivers don't perceive themselves as being 'slow'. Instead, they think they're being 'sensible'. They also return library books on time, recycle postage stamps that haven't been franked and give jars of home-made chutney as Christmas presents. So the driver will remain immune to all manifestations of your annoyance, probably while dropping his speed to a mere 5 miles per hour. You, meanwhile, will be provided with plenty of time to practise your anger management techniques.

Never stay too close behind a slow driver, because another of this group's characteristics is a tendency to brake unexpectedly and for no apparent reason. You will then crash into the back of the car ahead and be liable for any damage caused to both vehicles.

If you're a slow driver: spare a thought for other road users, move over to the hard shoulder and give them plenty of opportunities to overtake.

Two other points relating to speed:

- For some reason, anyone, male or female, who wears a hat while behind a wheel will drive very, very slowly (although, if it's a baseball cap, the opposite is true). Next time you're on the road, see how often hat wearers travel at a snail's pace.

There's no explanation why this should be the case; it just is.

⤙ Always get out of the way of a white van. It will be driven at terrifying speed by a boy so young that he's barely started to shave and is hunched low over the wheel. If you don't let him pass at once, he'll sit so close on your tail that you'll be able to lip-read his scornful abuse in your rear-view mirror. As insurance companies can confirm, all young men are liable to drive too fast. Members of the same high-risk group also frequently confuse the white van they're driving for a high-powered sports car.

MOBILE PHONES

Naturally you believe yourself to be a driver capable of holding an animated conversation on the mobile phone with your office receptionist while negotiating a tricky corner, lighting a cigarette and changing the radio station. Unfortunately, as with speed limits, the law believes otherwise and it holds the upper hand (both of your own being otherwise engaged in holding the phone, cig-

It's so important to leave one's hands free for the obscene gestures

arette and the steering wheel). Therefore, if you're inclined to use your mobile phone a lot while driving, it's advisable to buy a hands-free set. Alternatively, you could discover that answering every call at once really isn't necessary; mobile phones have been provided with a convenient facility to take messages.

MUSIC

If you're an adolescent male – or simply wish you were – you'll want to drive around your local town centre, no matter how bad the weather, with all windows in the car fully open and some drum 'n' bass tracks pumping out at an ear-shattering level. If you're anyone else, you'll observe these antics with disapproval.

Advice to adolescent males: your vehicle is not a moving nightclub, it's raining and you're going to get wet, and furthermore your taste in music is execrable.

Advice to anyone else: yes, the noise is horrendous but they're adolescent males so what else would you expect? Save yourself the trouble of getting annoyed as it will make no difference. Furthermore, in another year or two they'll have grown out of this phase – to be replaced by another generation whose taste is even more terrible.

ADDITIONAL CONSIDERATIONS

It's probably best not to assume the driver of the car coming towards you is a mind-reader. If planning to make a turn, use your indicator (the driver of the car behind will appreciate this too).

When turning right at a traffic junction, hook around the car turning to your left. You learnt this rule before taking the driving test (and then promptly forgot it afterwards).

Many people will be surprised to learn that seat belts – particularly those for passengers in the back – are not, like leather-covered steering wheels or teak-veneer dashboards, just another decorative feature of the car's internal fit-out. They serve a practical purpose as well. Find out what that is (and observe the law) by strapping yourself in.

When halted at traffic lights on the way to work, don't regard the lull as an opportunity to apply your morning make-up. The lights will change, the driver behind will blow his horn and you'll get such a shock the mascara brush will become embedded in your eye, requiring surgery for its removal.

In rush hour traffic, never stop in a yellow box. Without fail, when the lights turn red you'll be faced with the wrath of a juggernaut driver whose path has been blocked – by you. This country already has a monarch. You cannot, therefore, be King of the Road.

Travel Manners

You'll travel with a lighter heart, if not with lighter luggage, provided you understand the following points.

Unless you own a private jet, there's absolutely nothing glamorous about travel. It's just a necessarily tedious means of transporting yourself from one spot on the globe to another. Necessity and glamour have nothing in common, ergo: travel is not glamorous.

'Hell', wrote Jean-Paul Sartre, 'is other people.' Other people, that is, milling around an airport departure terminal. Derive some crumb of comfort from the thought that while this existential hell is no more than an intermittent experience for you, it's a way of life for all the people who work in the building. They will, therefore, respond poorly to demands that cannot be met. If you desperately want an aisle seat in row seven, get to the check-in counter early enough to secure it. Otherwise accept that the only place left on your long-haul flight is going to be next to the toilets. Customers who are polite at check-in are more likely to get what they want or, at the very least, less likely to get a seat next to the toilets. (*Tip:* Read the name written on an identity badge and use it when asking staff if they are having a hellish day, without fail, the answer will be yes.) Occasionally, your ingratiating efforts could even be rewarded with an upgrade.

Self check-in is by far the speediest way to travel as it cuts out queuing. An electronic ticket is all you need.

Some of us travel light, some of us travel as though we're fleeing political oppression and have to take with us as many of our belongings as possible. If you're one of the second group, even before leaving home accept that you'll be asked to pay extra for your luggage. Never argue with check-in staff over the size and weight of your bags; this is a fight you cannot win, primarily because they'll have heard every plea/argument/excuse before. Probably from the passenger immediately ahead of you and he was eventually forced to surrender ten pieces of luggage. Besides, having lost the argument, not only will you then be ordered to hand over all your bags at check-in but you'll also be advised that the last remaining seat on your long-haul flight is next to the toilets.

An old army maxim: any group can only move as fast as its slowest member. Don't be the person who delays a flight's departure because you're still finishing a drink in the airport bar when everyone else has boarded the plane.

Without fail, on every flight there are a number of people who, having managed to find their way to the airport, discovered the relevant check-in area, thoroughly explored Duty Free and even arrived at the appropriate boarding gate on time, revert to a state of helpless imbecility as soon as they board the plane. This condition manifests itself in an inability to work out where they are supposed to sit. Unless it's a free-seating flight, your seat number is on your boarding pass stub and it corresponds to a number on the ceiling above each row of seats.

Now, that wasn't so difficult to work out, was it?

Also on every flight at least a quarter of the passengers will block everyone else's progress for several minutes while they place carry-on luggage in the overhead locker and ignore regular requests relayed over the tannoy to step in from the aisle. At least one couple will engage in an extensive debate over whether a cardigan should be taken out of a bag for the journey or not. Items of clothing and magazines will pass back and forth, while on the steps of the plane outside – where it will almost certainly be raining – a queue of irate passengers starts to form. Elsewhere on board, several single travellers – always those seated closest to the window and therefore liable to cause the greatest amount of disruption – will regularly need to check items of luggage they had earlier stowed away. Before you board the plane, decide what you'll need during the flight.

It is an indisputable rule of travel that the coats and jackets you carefully folded and placed overhead will emerge looking as though they had been left lying on the floor for the flight's duration. The reason? Another passenger has managed to squeeze into the same locker not only his overnight bag and more bottles of duty-free whiskey than he is legally permitted to carry, but also a life-size replica of a donkey. Something had to suffer and it was your coat.

The plane will barely have taken off before the seat immediately in front of you reclines to a near-horizontal position. This is particularly aggravating when you are about to eat lunch and would rather not do so off your lap. You can now buy, over the internet, a gadget that stops the seat in front from reclining. However, some airlines have already banned this device.

If a passenger in the row ahead does unexpectedly and inconveniently invade your space, politely make your feelings clear and the seat will usually revert to its upright position. Should that not happen, repeatedly cross and uncross your legs, each time bringing one – or both – of your feet into contact with the back of the seat in front. Its padding is sure to be thin and this activity will cause enormous discomfort to the passenger who has inconvenienced you.

Want to recline your own seat? Wait until all drinks and meals have been finished and then ask the passenger behind if you can put your seat back. He/she will be so astounded by this freak outbreak of courtesy that no objection will be made.

If you like to sleep while travelling, train yourself to do so in an upright position. Otherwise you'll slump over your neighbour and wake up to find you've left a line of unappealing drool on the shoulder of a stranger. There is a small inflatable cushion widely available that fits around your neck and keeps your head straight. It looks silly but better that than having to pay someone else's dry-cleaning bill.

On long-haul flights, by the time the trolley reaches your row, your choice of meal will no longer be available. Rather than settle for beef when you really wanted chicken, declare yourself a vegetarian or claim some other dietary distinction when booking the ticket. As an extra bonus, you'll discover these meals are always served first. Alternatively, bring your own picnic – it's almost certain to taste better than what's offered by the airline.

As soon as the plane lands, the people seated in the back row will immediately leap up and unload all their possessions from the overhead lockers, even though at least fifteen minutes must pass before they can hope to disembark. Likewise, ignoring instructions from the cabin crew that mobile phones should not be used until passengers are inside the airport terminal, the man in the seat next to you will switch on his phone and begin a loud conversation with the announcement, 'We've just landed.'

OTHER TRAVEL NOTES
Parents of small children please note: a plane, train or coach is

not an activity playground. Try to keep your offspring under control, do not allow them to race each other up and down the centre aisle, and discourage them from repeatedly kicking the back of the seat in front.

There are some earphones that allow no noise to escape, but those aren't the kind supplied on aircraft. If your neighbours want to listen to the same music as you, they can put on their own earphones rather than hear it second-hand from yours.

Want to see yourself in the following day's newspapers? Argue with the on-board cabin crew and there'll be a posse of police – plus one or two representatives of the local media – waiting to greet you at the flight's destination. Being charged with air rage is not dignified.

The Outdoor Life

While it's possible to encourage good manners and courtesy in private houses and controlled environments, trying to do this in public locations poses a serious challenge. What follows next, therefore, is not so much advice on how to behave as a warning of what to expect whenever you venture outdoors.

PETS

Parks should be restful places where you can contemplate nature. But often nature, in the guise of a dauntingly large dog, prefers to contemplate you. Dog owners don't seem to understand that a park visitor left cowering behind the laurel shrubbery will have failed to appreciate that their Rottweiler was only trying to be friendly. In all public places, dogs ought to be kept on a lead. Without this restraint, they are inclined to investigate strangers' legs as potential posts against which to urinate. Wet trousers are not comfortable and, in any case, private clubs exist for people who enjoy that kind of thing.

For reasons of public hygiene, when walking your dog it shows consideration to bring a bag for pooper scooping. Concrete footpaths don't need to be fertilized, so use the bag on every necessary occasion – and not just when you think someone else is looking.

Outside the home, all pets need to be kept in check (although an exception can be made for tortoises and hamsters). So too do children, especially those inclined to treat the local park as an extension of their back garden. Any unbridled enthusiasm for running around shouting, kicking footballs (or each other), pulling up plants and the like must be curbed. Leads for children are not permitted, so alternative methods will be needed. Parents, like pet owners, are inclined not to notice the effect their offspring have on others. Until, that is, they receive an official complaint via a member of the local police force.

PEOPLE

Wide open spaces such as parks attract two kinds of people: those who want to sit there in silence; and those who see it as the ideal spot for a game of five-a-side soccer. These two kinds of people are incompatible and can never share the same outlook – or even the same open space. Force of numbers eventually decides which side is the winner, although it takes a lot of old-age pensioners to outmanoeuvre a five-a-side soccer team.

Similar conflicts are evident on seaside beaches, where soccer players engage in a never-resolved turf war with frisbee throwers. The only certain loser will be anyone hoping to enjoy a quiet afternoon in the sun, namely you. Expect large amounts of sand to be kicked about the beach, noisy disputes over scored points and a ball (or frisbee) to land regularly on your towel.

Participants in these games are males aged between twelve

and twenty. Their behaviour will become noisier and rowdier if there are girls of a similar age in the vicinity. While you are driven into a frenzy of irritation by the boys' games, the girls will pay them no attention whatsoever.

WATER SPORTS

The other threats to your peace at the seaside come from speed-boats and the various sporting activities taking place on the water itself. Participants in all such activities regard swimmers as Luddite-like nuisances who should be cleared out of the sea as soon as possible. For your own safety, sooner or later you will agree with them. The only place where it is still possible to swim without losing either your temper or, quite literally, your head is a pool.

An additional hazard from the likes of speedboats and jet skis is noise. Everyone agrees that noise is a modern pollutant. But, like any other form of pollution, no one will ever admit to being responsible for its creation. Nevertheless, we're all regularly assailed by aural mugging and, like any other victim of an unprovoked attack, the effect is to leave us disoriented and upset. Sadly, the rest of the world's population will never share your fabulous good taste in music; one man's Maria Callas is always going to be another man's nails scratched down a black-board. Try to remember this point, together with the location of the volume control dial on your radio/CD player.

Pavement Peeve

Noise pollution is just one of many forms of disregard for the interests of other people within a communal environment. Road rage has been a widely reported phenomenon among car drivers but to date less attention has been paid to a related condition, which could be categorized as pavement peeve. Outbreaks of this can occur on any of the following occasions:

- ❧ When a group of friends amble along together, taking up the entire width of a narrow pavement and allowing no one else to pass.
- ❧ When an untidy queue of commuters waiting for a bus oblige passers-by to step onto the road (and into the path of an oncoming bus).
- ❧ When the person walking in front of you suddenly pulls up short to greet someone coming in the opposite direction.
- ❧ When a cyclist decides the footpath is a more convenient passageway than the adjacent road.

Shops

It is generally considered good manners to hold shop doors open for anybody who falls into one or more of the following categories: the elderly, the disabled, women (especially if pregnant and/or pushing a pram).

Always shop with a list written in advance. This will prevent you from wandering aimlessly around your local centre for several hours. Unless, of course, that's precisely what you planned to do, in which case you're a bored teenager and it's Saturday.

No matter how rude or disinterested they might appear, always be pleasant to staff in shops. You won't necessarily receive better service but your blood pressure will remain lower. Never complain directly to a member of staff who you think is failing to do his/her job properly. Instead, take out a piece of paper and a pen and ask for the staff member's name and that of the manager. For further effect, you might like ostentatiously to note down the time and date. The result of this activity tends to be a rapid improvement in the quality of service. But if this doesn't occur, you now have the necessary information for composing a strongly worded letter of complaint to the shop when back at home.

Understand that sales staff will always be more interested in talking to each other than to you. After all, you don't know Simon from Soft Furnishings and what he said in the pub last night.

Cinemas, Theatres, Concert Halls

Mobile phones should not, of course, be used in places of public entertainment such as cinemas and theatres. Despite repeated requests before the start of the performance, one member of the audience will fail to switch off his/her mobile phone. Accordingly, this will ring at a critical moment in the film or play. Everyone will sigh audibly and wonder who could be guilty of such a shocking lack of consideration. You will do likewise, at least until you realize that the ringing phone is yours.

RAPT SILENCE

Is the correct response when listening to classical music. Nevertheless, some people persist in the belief that they should greet the concert's quieter passages with a crescendo of coughing. They then engage in the following sequence of events: a series of whispered apologies; a frantic rustling through pockets or handbags; and, finally, the sound of a boiled sweet being unwrapped. One of their number, possibly selected in the foyer beforehand, will decide that, rather than disturb the performance any further, it is best to leave the hall. This exit involves an entire row of the audience standing up to let out the cougher.

CLAPPING

In the wrong place at classical concerts is considered a heinous offence. No matter how much you're enjoying the performance, never clap between movements but save your applause for the end of the entire work. If in doubt, don't clap at all. The rest of the audience will then conclude that you must be a music critic.

AUDIENCE RESPONSES
Even if you dislike the music, opera is satisfying because it's the one field of performance where booing is not only permitted but almost obligatory. Singers are rarely booed unless they're very bad (i.e. worse than you in the shower after a late night) but no production can be considered a complete success unless its designer and/or director is faced with a hostile audience when taking curtain calls.

If you want to give the impression of being an opera devotee, learn that male singers are greeted with shouts of 'bravo' and their female equivalents with 'brava'. Unfortunately, things then become much more complicated because in many operas there are women playing male parts and vice versa, so you might prefer just to call out, 'Well done.'

TALKING
Is allowed at rock concerts. Allowed but not possible because the amplification is too loud to hear what anyone is saying. Here is an invaluable opportunity to brush up on your lip-reading skills.

Although you won't be permitted to smoke at an indoor rock concert, you will be allowed to carry a lighter. This is to hold over your head while any slow or anthemic number is being played.

If you're still in your teens, you'll be expected to dance energetically to the music (at least until a member of the security staff orders you to sit down). Once you're over the age of twenty, the correct response at a rock concert is a gentle swaying of your body and an expression of rapt attention on your face. The latter suggests deep engagement with the music, whereas you'll actually be worrying whether you parked the car in a safe place.

FOOD AND DRINK

At the theatre, concert hall or opera house, consumption of anything more substantial than a boiled sweet (see above) is frowned upon. Nevertheless, one group of pensioners meeting for their annual outing will have brought with them a box of chocolates. Once the play or concert begins, they can be identified by the sound of rustling that emanates from their row as denture-wearing members of the group struggle in the semi-gloom to avoid selecting anything with a hard centre.

Although the comfort of a double vodka might help to get you through a performance, you won't be allowed to take your glass into the auditorium. This explains why there's always such a frenzy at the theatre bar during the interval as sections of the audience attempt to achieve a semi-comatose condition before being summoned back to their seats for the second act.

At the cinema, on the other hand, eating and drinking are encouraged, as indicated by the plethora of concession stands you'll have to pass after buying your ticket. It's important to understand that without your purchase of an extra-large tub of popcorn, two fizzy drinks and a bag of sweets, admission charges to the cinema would have to be raised, or every film shown only for a few days. Notice how the audience at an art film rarely consumes anything more than a bottle of mineral water between them, whereas during a commercial film of unsurpassed violence, the audience eats enough to wipe out famine in central Africa. Cinemas obviously depend on their sales of junk food, which is why art films always close before you get a chance to see them, while the violent ones you don't want to watch are sure to run for months and months.

CINEMA SEATING
It's an unwritten but widely understood rule of cinema attendance that you should never sit immediately next to people
who've already taken their seats. Instead, you're expected to
leave a single space between yourself and them. This ensures
that couples arriving less than ten minutes before the film starts
will be unable to sit together. Anyone who sits down next to a
stranger in a half-filled cinema can expect to be regarded as a
potential menace to society.

In every cinema, one seat remains vacant. It is the middle
seat in the middle row and will be filled only when the film has
begun and the maximum number of people can be disrupted
by a late arrival.

It is bad manners to talk in the cinema. Particularly if you've
seen the film before and are revealing details of the plot.

The Gym

Unless the gym has been installed in the basement of your
home, there are likely to be other people present. Which means
manners still matter – even when you're dressed in not much
more than a pair of running shorts.

CLOTHES
Wear enough of them and make sure they hold any potentially
volatile parts of your anatomy firmly in place. On the running
machine, for example, only your legs ought to be in motion.
There's a wide range of support sportswear that can make sure
this is the case.

Dress in a way that ensures both physical and psychological

comfort. If you insist on wearing skimpy or revealing clothes in the gym, expect to attract attention whether you want it or not. Staring is always bad manners, of course, but frankly what else are people going to do when you step out of the changing room in a micro-strip of Lycra? Likewise, should you be uncomfortable with other gym members casting an eye over your selection of tattoos or piercings, an easy way to avoid this is by keeping all body ornamentation under cover.

It's fine to wear old clothes to the gym, provided they're completely clean. The exception is sports footwear. After a certain amount of heavy use (between three and six months, depending on how often you exercise), these not only become potentially hazardous for the wearer but they also start to smell. Invest regularly in a new pair of running shoes.

CLEANLINESS
Consider showering before, as well as after, you use the gym. It's now half past five and you've had a stressful day at work – a pre-workout shower will not only relax you, but also wash away any odours that have built up since the morning. Body odour: be conscious that you may not notice your own, but other people will. Enough said. Equally, avoid dousing yourself with strong perfume before going to the gym; physical exercise will only make its scent even more pungent.

SWEAT
Unless you're of the 'gently glowing' persuasion, physical exercise will cause you to sweat. Contrary to what advertisements might suggest, even the most powerful anti-perspirant can't compete with fifteen minutes on the rowing machine. While there's nothing you can do about breaking into a sweat, you can make sure no evidence of this is left behind. Once you've finished with any piece of equipment, wipe it down. Bring a small

clean towel with you for this purpose – it's also handy for dabbing any moisture off your brow.

TIDINESS

Leave all equipment as you'd wish to find it. As well as removing any pools of sweat from the seat and surrounding areas, you should put weights back tidily and clear any programmes set on a machine.

Don't hog machines. Other than around three o'clock on a mid-week afternoon, your gym is likely to be a busy place with heavy demand for the piece of equipment you're currently using. So use it only for a set amount of time, clean up fast and then move on. Every gym has one member who, having finished his workout (and yes, this person is, without fail, a man) stays draped over the machine breathing heavily and displaying no awareness that other people might want to take his place. An infallible rule of the gym; there are never enough machines to meet demand and there's always a queue to use the most popular ones.

SHOWING OFF

Efforts to impress other members of the gym invariably lead to one result: serious injury. When exercising, focus on your programme, not on letting everyone else in the vicinity know how fabulously fit you are. Showing off is more likely to win you glares of irritation than glances of approval.

Remember that the gym is a communal environment. Above all, this means no excessive grunting. Keep your workout quiet – no one needs to know how far you're pushing yourself. Frankly, no one probably cares anyway.

The gym is not a pick-up joint; why do you think bars were invented? Besides, you're sure to make a better impression on the object of your interest when you're not dressed in a sweat-drenched T-shirt.

12. Romantic Life

You're as likely to spot your ideal partner across the aisle of a supermarket as across a dinner table. There's no perfect place for these encounters. But it remains true that the chances of connecting with someone suitable are much higher if you're both somewhere that reflects your shared interests. Which is why advice columnists suggest that the best way to meet new people is by joining clubs or taking evening classes. It's also why so many of us meet our future partners through a mutual friend.

What's absolutely certain is that neither your social circle nor your romantic life will ever improve if you remain at home alone. If you want to get yourself someone special, then get out

How's my breath?

there and mingle. By the way, everything in this chapter applies to both genders regardless of sexual orientation.

Prelude: On Being Single

A BRIEF NOTE ON COMPLAINING ABOUT YOUR SINGLE STATUS

Don't. It has to be one of the most boring subjects of conversation, the fictional Bridget Jones did it better (and more amusingly) than you'll ever manage and it certainly won't make you more alluring to potential partners.

THE BENEFITS OF BEING SINGLE

Despite your romantic life being under discussion here, appreciate the merits of the single status. These include:

- Being the cause of envy among all your married/settled friends.
- Watching whatever you want, whenever you want, on TV.
- Eating as much garlic as you like without fear of the consequences.
- Not having to share a bathroom.
- Never being obliged to suffer someone else's maddening habit of abstractedly humming out of tune.

A HARSH TRUTH

Other than in the pages of romantic novels, there isn't necessarily a perfect soul mate for each of us out there just waiting to be discovered.

ANOTHER HARSH TRUTH

After the first heady days of falling in love, your romantic life will demand hard work and dedication from you if it's going to have a long-term future. Decide now whether you're prepared for all that.

MEETING YOUR MATCH

If you really want a romantic life, don't be old-fashioned. You no longer have to wait around for the village elder to introduce you to your future partner or for Mr Darcy to invite Miss Bennett for a turn on the dancefloor. There are alternative options, particularly when neither your friends nor your social life appear to be delivering prospective mates. Take charge of the situation and look at various contemporary options, such as meeting people through dating agencies, personal advertisements and the internet. Contrary to widespread belief, these aren't only suitable for the congenitally useless and you've certainly no right to condemn them without first trying what they've got to offer.

Meeting Someone for the First Time

If you've arranged to meet somebody through a dating agency or the internet, note these easy-to-follow rules:

-➤ Always meet in a public place, such as a cafe or bar. Consider this first encounter as a preliminary inspection and keep it brief. You can always arrange to meet again. Also, understand that the person you meet probably won't correspond exactly to the person described in the personal advertisement or internet chatroom. So a little exaggeration took place, so what? After all, you either added several inches to your height or deducted several years from your age. It's called Presenting Yourself in the Best Possible Light. On the other hand, if he claimed to be six foot two with model good looks and an athletic build but turns out to be five foot nothing and only good for modelling in an advertisement for dog food (with him playing the part of the dog), then you're entitled to lodge a complaint under the terms of the Trades Description Act.

- Having agreed to meet another person, you must keep the appointment, no matter how bad your last-minute attack of nerves. Never do either of the following: arrive at the agreed spot, decide you don't like the look of the person you're supposed to be meeting and leave without even saying hello. Meet the person, then excuse yourself within a few minutes and leave without saying goodbye. Both these actions are cowardly and cruel – not to mention terribly bad-mannered. Imagine how you'd feel if someone did the same thing to you.

- It's permissible (and even advisable) to tell a friend what you're doing and arrange that you get a call on your mobile phone after half an hour. If the person you've met has proven to be completely hopeless, this call allows you to make your excuses and leave. ('I'm sorry, but my mother's fallen down the stairs and broken both her legs' or something similar will do the trick.)

- If you give the person you've just met your address, telephone number or email details, prepare for the possibility that these will be used. Be cautious how much information you divulge to strangers. This isn't rudeness, just common sense and a great way to avoid acquiring obsessive stalkers.

- Be honest – about yourself, about what you're looking for, and about the person you're meeting for the first time. If the spark isn't there, then it isn't there. The sooner you say so, the better for both of you. At the same time, try to be considerate; this encounter probably hasn't been easy for either of you.

◆ Even if you feel an immediate spark of attraction, don't hesitate to make further enquiries about someone you've met via a dating agency or the internet. Likewise, don't be upset if the other person asks around about you. In romantic terms, this is the same as looking for professional references; it shows that there's a strong interest in offering you the position.

First Dates

WHO SHOULD ASK?
Probably whoever's the braver of the two. The old rule of a man asking a woman hasn't much validity any more and besides, what about when it's a same-sex scenario? So, if you're interested in seeing someone for a date, forget about any archaic role-playing and make the suggestion.

HOW TO ACCEPT?
You'll find the word 'yes' is usually sufficient. If you accept the invitation to go on a date, understand that the person making the offer will be entitled to choose where and when your meeting takes place. Ideally, your opinions should be taken into account but unless the date involves something extreme like abseiling down the side of a mountain, good manners oblige you to go along with whatever's being offered.

HOW TO REFUSE?
Immediately and politely and with the intention of causing your spurned suitor as little embarrassment as possible. You're not under any obligation to provide an explanation for your refusal and it's usually wiser not to give one.

THE DATE

Once you've accepted the invitation, don't pin too many expectations on a first date. The request was to have lunch, for heaven's sake, not take a trip up the aisle together. The first date serves only one function: helping the two of you to get to know one another better. Quite how much better is entirely up to you. On a first date, you're entitled to say no to anything, from a second helping of vegetables to the suggestion that you go back to his/her place for a drink.

First dates are like actors' auditions where you're hoping to win the role without being completely confident that it's the right one for you. It's understandable that both parties involved will be more nervous than usual. Try to do whatever you can to ease the other person's nervousness even if your feelings are much the same. A first date is almost always awkward for the two of you because at the back of your minds lurks the same question: is there going to be a second date?

During the encounter, be enthusiastic but not too eager, talkative but not to the point where your date never gets a chance to speak. Nervousness is inclined to make many of us garrulous but a first date shouldn't be treated as an opportunity for you to deliver a monologue. It's a conversation during which two people discover how much – or how little – they have in common.

What if, during the course of the meeting, it turns out that the two of you actually have nothing in common and a second date is destined never to occur? You can make this fact plain without stating it explicitly. Put all positive body language into reverse: undilate the pupils of your eyes; stop licking your lips; keep your fingers away from your hair. But remain polite and retain at least a semblance of interest in your date. This is particularly important when the other person invited you out and is now paying, in more ways than one, for the privilege. In effect, what you need to do is subtly but unmistakably change your role from being a date to being a good guest.

A DÉBUT DATE WILL NOT GO WELL IF YOU

- Talk only about yourself.
- Speak endlessly about your exes. (Particularly if you've nothing kind to say about any of them – who'd want to become one of that number?)
- Boast of your successes, whether professional, personal or sexual.
- Are too self-deprecating.
- Fail to ask the other person about him/herself.
- Can't make him/her laugh at least once (humour is a great bonder).
- Keep looking around the room.

On that last point, it can't be stressed enough that when you're out with one person, you should act as though there were nobody else in the world of any importance to you. A wandering eye indicates wandering attention.

SILENCES

Often occur on a first date. These are quite different from the silences you observe between two people who've been married for thirty years. A characteristic of early dates is awkwardness but this can be avoided by having enough to talk about. It may seem too calculated, but there's no harm in preparing a few topics of conversation ahead of your meeting. Read the paper, listen to the news, think about what was being discussed at work today. What are the subjects that everyone else seems to be talking about, whether the latest TV reality show or the English premiership results? If still stuck for something to say, ask your date questions about him/herself. All of us find ourselves the most scintillating topic of conversation.

Post-First Date

If you're the one who's been taken out, good manners oblige you to show adequate gratitude, even when you've no intention of repeating the experience. You don't plan to see the other person again? Don't risk a telephone call but instead send a pleasant note or email expressing thanks for the hospitality while making it clear that a second date is not, and never will be, under consideration.

The best way to do this is by adopting a neutral tone and ending your note with a polite but firm brush-off along the lines of, 'It was nice to have met you and I wish you every success in your career in bathroom sanitation. Yours sincerely …'. That should get across the message that you've no future together. Let the other person down gently, no matter how irritating you found his/her attention.

You do want a second date? Your thanks will be much more effusive (and you certainly won't end your note with the words 'yours sincerely'). But never be too keen at the start of any relationship. Keenness can easily be confused with desperation. And desperation is not a winning formula.

GETTING IN TOUCH AFTER A FIRST DATE
Do so within twenty-four hours and you're liable to appear a little too needy. Leave it for more than three days and you're likely to appear indifferent. Sometime between these two extremes is best. Despite the enormous number of books written on the subject of dating, there are no absolute rules in this area other than the obligation to remember courtesy. The advice that women shouldn't reply to a phone call for a weekend date if it's made after Wednesday might, just possibly, be good tactics in the campaign to snare a male partner but it's also

bad manners. In addition, if it's one woman ringing another, that advice is just plain nonsense.

The Delicate Art of Seduction

At some point, perhaps at the end of your first date, possibly after several dates, you're likely to move from public to private surroundings. And there's a place for good manners even in the bedroom. In fact, the first point to make on this subject concerns the state of that room: it should be clean and tidy, as should the bed it contains. Avoid leaving clothes, especially dirty ones, lying around. Have the room well aired and odour free. On the night in question, your sheets ought to be clean even if your thoughts aren't.

SEVERAL OTHER HELPFUL POINTS
Think soft lighting – other than professional strippers, we're all inclined to be a bit self-conscious getting undressed in front of someone else for the first time. Think sufficient warmth – hot sex is less likely to happen in cold surroundings. Think comfort – not everyone will find your thin futon on the floor conducive to erotic pleasure.

BONUS POINTS WILL BE AWARDED FOR THE FOLLOWING
- Scented candles.
- The provision of a robe for your partner.
- A spare toothbrush.
- A hanger offered for his/her clothes (because even when ripped off in the first fit of passion they're going to be worn again the following morning).

What one/other/both of you should also have is adequate sexual protection. Carrying this at all times does not imply that you're a promiscuous tramp; it indicates that you quite correctly have your own – and your partner's – well-being in mind. Condoms are small and easily carried, they remain a reliable (although not infallible) method of avoiding unwanted pregnancies and they do a lot to stop the transmission of sexual diseases. On the subject of which, if you do have an STD of any kind, you're under an obligation to tell the other person before anything beyond conversation occurs between the pair of you.

It's impossible to arbitrate absolutely on what constitutes good sex between two people. And this task becomes even tougher when more than two are involved. However, what can be said with certitude on the subject is that practice frequently makes better, if not necessarily perfect.

The first time, therefore, will rarely see either party turn in an award-winning performance. Again, rather like a first date, the whole occasion can have the character of an audition – and even the best actors have been known to fluff those. Allowances should be made for nerves as well as for unfamiliarity with one another's bodies and specific likes/dislikes. Get to know these (which requires honesty, the basis of all successful relationships) and find out what does or doesn't work for each of you. This will help to ensure you have a mutually happy sex life. Enough said.

Hints for a Happy Courtship

Men: If you can possibly help it, when you and your partner are out together, avoid looking at other women (or men, depending on your preferences).

Women: Don't feel as though you're under an obligation to talk for two.

Men: Always compliment your partner on his/her appearance.

Women: Never ask your partner whether what you're wearing makes you look fat.

Men: Never answer the above question – whatever you say will be wrong.

Women: Learn to show some interest in the subjects that interest him. Or at least look as though you do.

Men: Ditto.

Women: If you ask for your partner's opinion or advice (on any subject), expect it to be given.

Men: No matter how long you've been together, regularly give your partner flowers.

Women: Don't mind if he never gives you flowers – it's not that important.

Men: Try to remember anniversaries (the first time you met, the date of your wedding, her birthday).

Both: Never criticize one another in public. To do so marks the beginning of the end. If you've problems together, sort them out in private.

How to Make a Relationship Last

- Continue to remember your manners.
- Be appreciative.
- Show gratitude for acts of kindness, no matter how small they are or how often they've been performed.
- Say please and thank you.
- Never take anything or anyone for granted. If you say you're going to telephone at a certain time or be in a certain place, stick to your word.
- Avoid allowing standards to slip. Remember who and what

you were when you first met your partner and stay that way.
↞ Don't become complacent, about yourself, about your boy/girlfriend, about your relationship.

A note on flirting: Some people feel a persistent desire to be found attractive. This is usually expressed through flirting. As a rule, the flirt requires no more than a brief and immediate response from the object of his/her attention. If you're that object, understand that the attention you're receiving is transitory and liable to be transferred, sooner or later, to someone else.

The same lesson needs to be learnt by anyone who's the boy/girlfriend of a flirt. Infuriating as you might find your partner's tendency to chat up the rest of the room, try to understand that this is no more than a personality trait, like being shy or untidy.

Flirts, on the other hand, ought to realize that their habit of constantly wooing any- and everyone can be misconstrued, not only by their partners but by the person with whom they're flirting. Particularly if you know your boy/girlfriend is driven close to insanity by your flirtatious tendencies, try to curb the instinct.

Romantic Life and Friends

When seeing someone new, only gradually introduce the object of your romantic interest into your social circle. Don't expect your friends to feel the same way about your boy/girlfriend as you do. If they did, they'd be going out with him/her instead of you. It's best not to ask friends' opinion of your partner. Should they want to tell you what they think, they will. And make sure you get to know your new partner's social world. There's something suspect about anyone whose friends are never introduced to you.

While you're modern, open-minded and untroubled by any conceivable permutation of coupling, other people – specifically your family and friends – won't necessarily share these liberal values. If you think they might be taken aback by your new partner – for reasons of gender, colour, age, animal species – break the news gently and be prepared for the possibility of dismay or even distaste.

Recognize that while the details of your personal life are always going to be a source of fascination and wonderment to you, others may not view them in quite the same light. Don't test your friends' patience by wanting to talk ad nauseam on the subject whenever you:

- Fall in or out of love.
- Have had a row with your boy/girlfriend.
- Discover he/she has cheated on you.
- Just don't understand why your chosen soul mate can't appreciate the merits of washing a teacup after it has been used.

If you need to have these kind of conversations regularly, it's worth investing in a good therapist who, unlike your friends, will be paid to listen to your wailings.

DON'T NEGLECT FRIENDS

No matter how much you're in love. They're the people you'll need most when the relationship encounters difficulties (as it invariably will) and they're much less likely to be available if you haven't been around for them in recent months due to your romantic entanglements. Make time for your friends now and they'll make time for you later.

EXPRESSING OPINIONS

Unless you've serious grounds for concern about a friend's new boy/girlfriend (he's got a criminal record/she's had three husbands all of whom died in mysterious circumstances) keep your opinions to yourself. Speak your mind, especially when it's of a critical caste, and you could find yourself not invited to the happy couple's wedding next year.

The same applies even when the pair have broken up. Under no circumstances perceive this as an opportunity to say what you really thought of your friend's ex; they might get back together again a week later. Even if this doesn't happen, the remarks you make will still imply criticism of your friend's judgment.

Be pleasant to a friend's new partner but not too pleasant too fast. If the relationship falters, your original friend will most likely need your support and this'll be harder to give should you have become equally close to the now-ex partner.

A note on PDAs – Public Displays of Affection or Anger: PDAs invariably provide everyone else with TMI (Too Much Information). As a result, they're to be discouraged. No matter how strong your feelings towards one another, never hit or hit on someone else in public. Teenagers replete with raging hormones and without a place to call their own can just about get away with putting on a demonstration of kissing prowess. The rest of you should either curb your feelings or find somewhere private where you can give full vent to them. The same goes for arguing in public; it indicates total self-absorption and a lack of consideration for the rest of us. In other words, it's bad manners.

One-Night Stands

The encounter is brief but it can be memorable, provided you don't shed your manners as quickly as your inhibitions. It's discourteous to complain about your partner's sexual perform-ance. The earth didn't move? Well, that's why this is called a one-night stand and not a lifetime commitment.

If asked to engage in practices that are beyond either your physical capabilities or your ethical boundaries, decisively refuse. Similarly, should you have any special requirements or skills of your own, state them. Who's capable of reading the mind, let alone the body, of someone they only met a few hours earlier? This isn't a good moment for coyness, so the more clearly both of you articulate your requirements, the more sat-isfactory the eventual outcome.

Regardless of how thrilling the experience promises to be, for the sake of your long-term health, insist on the use of con-traceptive protection. You're entitled to call a halt to all pro-ceedings if this isn't available.

After sex, always ask if you may stay the night, never pre-sume that you can. If, instead, you want to go back to your own home, say and do so. The excuse that you're a noisy snorer should permit a speedy exit. Likewise, if it's your home and you want to sleep alone, make this clear. Although in these circum-stances, the offer of a bed elsewhere in the house ought to be made. (Who's going to find a taxi at four o'clock in the morn-ing?) You opt to spend the night together? Don't take up most of the bed and don't hog the entire duvet.

The following morning act as you would in the company of any relative stranger – only with far fewer clothes. Always carry some form of breath-freshener with you; it's a godsend when greeting someone you barely know at eight o'clock. Serial one-nighters learn to travel with a disposable toothbrush. Unless invited to linger, have a shower (you're allowed to ask for a clean towel), eat any breakfast offered, convey your thanks and leave.

Should the two of you run into one another again, even if embarrassment is your overwhelming emotion, suppress the urge to ignore the other person – that's just rude. Simply acknowledge that you have met before – without going into the graphic details – and then, unless a second night together seems possible, move on.

And a final note for anyone who plans to host a one-night stand: try to change your sheets regularly, keep some contraceptives to hand, have croissants in the freezer and orange juice in the fridge. A carton of milk that hasn't passed its use-by date several weeks earlier is always nice too.

How to End Well

Complete honesty has to be the basis of all successful relationships so if it's not working, you ought to be honest about that too. However, before decisively calling time, ask yourself: is this a temporary glitch (and therefore perfectly normal, happens to everyone sooner or later) or something more serious? If you're absolutely convinced it's the latter, be frank with your partner and explain clearly why the relationship has ended.

Even if you've only been seeing each other for a couple of weeks, always end a relationship in person, not by cowardly means like a telephone call, text, email or letter. Or, worst of all, by silence and a refusal to respond to all efforts to contact you. Telling someone in person that your relationship is over won't be easy. However, it offers the best likelihood that you'll subsequently keep in touch, or at least retain good memories of one another.

If you're leaving for someone else, admit this from the start. You may think your justification for not telling the truth was kindness but it won't be viewed like that by anyone else. There's nothing worse than the other person finding out later that you were lying. That way lies vicious recriminations, shredded clothes, boiled bunnies – and worse.

Don't expect friendship to follow immediately afterwards – allow the healing process of time to do its work (and in the meantime, don't do or say anything to jeopardize the possibility that the two of you will become friends at some future date).

You're the person being left? Try to accept what has happened with as much grace and humour as you can muster (not much, probably). Recognize that you're feeling some pain (alright, a lot of pain). Don't complain about this in public; even your best friends will quickly grow tired of hearing about what a rat your former partner is. See a therapist if you really need to talk to someone about the experience. And, like falling in love or having a baby, remember you're not the first person to have gone through this process. It's normal, it happens to all of us, life goes on.

LINES THAT SHOULD NEVER BE USED WHEN ENDING A RELATIONSHIP

- 'It's not you, it's me.' (What are you? The scriptwriter for an afternoon soap opera?)
- 'I just need some space.' (Ditto.)
- 'There's nobody else.' (Especially when there is.)
- 'I'd really like us to stay friends.' (Keep that aspiration to yourself for the time being.)
- 'I don't think I'm ready for a relationship/commitment yet.' (So what were you doing in this one?)
- 'I hope we can be adult/civilized about this.' (Expect flying plates to follow a remark like that.)

Exes

After breaking up with somebody, unless one of you leaves the country and vows never to return, you're likely to meet again. When this happens, your immediate desire will probably be to turn around and walk speedily away in the opposite direction. This is not good behaviour. It's not sensible. It's certainly not grown-up. Take the proverbial deep breath, step forward brightly and greet your ex. Keep this first exchange short and keep it sweet. Then make your excuses, leave, and congratulate yourself on behaving, possibly for the first time ever, like an adult.

YOU MEET YOUR EX AT A PARTY

You and your ex will have been brought together either by accident or design (some friends forever try to effect reconciliations among members of their circle – usually with disastrous results). When it's a case of the former, the only tactic open to you is of the grin-and-bear-it variety. Be polite to the ex, spend as much time as courtesy demands and then turn your attention elsewhere. Should you discover that the entire event was staged to bring the two of you together, be grateful to those responsible; their intention was kind, no matter what the results. Should you and your ex move in the same social circles and be likely to bump into one another, you're entitled to ask who else will be coming to any parties given by mutual friends.

EX SEX

It happens with surprising regularity but with few consequences. It's rarely a prelude to the two of you getting back together; it's just sex with someone you already know. Try not to read too much into the event if it occurs, otherwise you'll give yourself a bad dose of regret and recrimination.

Don't bitch about your exes – ever. You'll sound bitter, repetitive and boring.

How to Conduct an Illicit Affair Successfully

You can't. Even if the affair remains known only to the two of you, the fact remains that it's illicit and therefore contains a fundamental dishonesty at its centre. There's a reason why the affair is illicit and, almost invariably, that reason is the presence of a third party – one/both of you has a partner who can't know what's going on. So what you've embarked upon is a course of deception that will subsequently involve not just the two of you but an ever-increasing number of other people as you're obliged to cover your tracks.

No matter how much gratification of the senses is involved, illicit affairs can never be entirely satisfactory because they can never be entirely honest. In addition, they come with the strong possibility that someone will be badly hurt. That person could be you.

Always remember the adage that a man who marries his mistress creates a job vacancy. If the person with whom you're having the affair wasn't faithful to his/her partner, what makes you think he/she'll be faithful to you?

What to do if you learn or realize that one of your friends is having an illicit affair? As in other circumstances where you acquire unpleasant information that you weren't supposed to have (you find out that a fellow worker in the office is downloading pornography from the internet or somebody you know turns out to be a kleptomaniac) your response depends on your own moral code and on how much you want to become involved in another person's life. Be aware that by choosing to become involved, you mightn't improve circumstances and could find yourself being branded a troublemaker and meddler. Probably the best course is to distance yourself from the person having the affair, explaining, if you must, why you're doing this (preferably without sounding like a prude or a prig).

Should you tell a friend if you discover that his/her partner is having an affair? Should you ever give someone seriously bad news? Here's an instance where there are no absolutes and you'll need to weigh up the consequences of your actions in advance. For example, your friend may already know that his/her partner regularly has affairs on the side and is prepared to live with this (think of the late MP Alan Clark and his wife). Or what had been a long-standing and happy relationship could now come to an end as a result of what you've done. Carefully weigh up the pros and cons and consider the broader picture before you do or say anything.

13. Addictive Substances

Increasingly, smokers are in a minority – and a dying one at that. They don't have any moral right on their side. Nobody's under an obligation to tolerate their addiction, especially since it's known to be the cause of many terminal illnesses. And clutching a cigarette doesn't transform anyone into Cary Grant or Audrey Hepburn.

Nicotine

Should you ask for permission to smoke in company? Yes, of course, always. If you're refused permission, accept this.

Keep your apologies for smoking to a minimum. Most of us understand that it's not altogether your fault. We will, however, not forgive you for going on about how sorry you are for smoking and how it's a disgusting habit and how you've tried to give up several times already and how the patches really didn't work for you and how you've an appointment with a hypnotherapist next week. Please, before we're driven to distraction (and to cigarettes), just light up and shut up.

Bring your own cigarettes with you. No cadging a smoke from someone else. This particularly applies to people who are prone to announcing, 'I'm not really a smoker,' before they light a cigarette taken from a packet that's not their own.

If you're a smoker at a party in a non-smoking house, try to do without cigarettes altogether. That's what you have to do everywhere else. But if abstinence only makes your heart beat fonder, quietly excuse yourself and step outdoors for your nicotine fix. You'll probably find yourself joined by half the party (and smokers always seem to have the most amusing conversations on these occasions). If the weather's vile, thoughtful hosts should provide a room in which smoking is allowed.

One last detail for the smoking guest; should you light up on someone else's property, please don't just toss away your butt when you've finished. There's something intensely irritating about the discovery of cigarette ends casually discarded into a flower-bed.

Smokers inviting other people to their home ought to be aware that the odour of nicotine lingers long after a cigarette's been stubbed out (just ask anyone who was ever caught smoking at school). Your living-room's liable to have the aroma of a stale ashtray. Open plenty of windows in advance of visitors and let in some fresh air (preferably don't use one of those so-called 'fresheners' that'll make the entire house smell like a cheap boiled sweet).

Reformed smokers: take the zeal somewhere else. Nobody cares to hear your story – again.

Alcohol

Is agreed to be responsible for enormous problems in our society. These include domestic violence, serious illness and premature death, work absenteeism, poverty and crime. Alcohol, of itself, causes none of these to occur but excessive consumption can be, and is, responsible for increasing their occurrence.

Moderate consumption, on the other hand, brings its own benefits. Medical research has shown that a certain amount of red wine is good for the heart. That certain amount, by the way, is less than you might think, or like. Alcohol also helps many of us to relax and to enjoy better the food that it accompanies.

Be aware of the effects of alcohol – on yourself and on others. If you're prone to drinking too much, or to turn nasty having done so, clearly you ought to seek help.

- *Drinkers:* Don't press drink on someone who doesn't want it. There are bound to be reasons why your offer of a pint was turned down. You might be told what these are, but not necessarily. In any case, 'no thanks' means just that. It's not a coy way of seeking further proposals.

- *Non-drinkers:* You're under no obligation to explain your abstinence and probably shouldn't unless asked to do so. Drinkers are often left feeling inexplicably guilty or degenerate in the presence of a teetotaller. Certainly, as a non-drinker you've no special entitlement to revel in a state of moral superiority.

- *Drinkers:* Understand the effect alcohol has on your character. And that your conversation, while you believe it to be growing steadily more fascinating, will become correspondingly less comprehensible to non-drinkers. Try not to annoy them with this.

- *Non-drinkers:* Unless you've the temperament of a saint, several hours spent in the company of drinkers can feel like several days. That's the effect alcohol has when you're not the person consuming it. If you find this to be the case, keep your time with heavy drinkers to a minimum.

- *Drinkers:* If one of your number is the fruit juice-drinking designated driver, don't abuse this person's charitable nature. All fruit juice ought to be free and you should let the d.d. demonstrate his/her abilities behind the steering wheel before it's four o'clock and the last nightclub has closed.

~ *Non-drinkers:* Don't proselytize. There's nothing inherently wrong with alcohol, only with its abuse.

~ *Drinkers:* Don't booze in an alcohol-free household. Also, you shouldn't bring alcohol to hosts who don't/won't drink it themselves. If you have to drink something with an alcoholic kick while all around you are quenching their thirst on herbal tea, slip away and have a shot of vodka, which has the advantage of being odourless. On the other hand, if you're really that desperate for a drink, maybe it's time to consider making contact with AA.

While rarely attractive or amusing, drunkenness is extremely common. Unless you took a vow in early childhood never to touch alcohol, you'll almost certainly have become drunk at least once. The likelihood is that when this occurred you made a spectacle of yourself and afterwards wished the whole thing had never happened – not least because your mortification was grimly accompanied by a raging hangover. What often makes this experience still worse is that it has taken place at a party and that you, therefore, believe yourself disgraced in the eyes of your hosts and the other guests.

There are, of course, degrees of drunkenness and disreputable conduct. You became much more voluble than usual or fell asleep at the dinner table? A phone call or written note of apology to the hosts ought to be enough to ensure forgiveness.

On the other hand, if you vomited over the carpet, made a pass at one guest or physically assaulted another, then greater evidence of contrition will be required. You may need to ask forgiveness, not just from your hosts, but from the rest of the party as well.

If there's been any damage done to property – clothing

soiled, glass broken – offer to pay whatever's necessary. Act with speed; no matter how ashamed you feel, apologize the next day for your actions – the longer you leave acknowledging your mistake, the greater time is left for others to develop a sense of grievance against you.

Avoid making excuses of the 'It was a chemical reaction to medication I'm taking' or 'I've never behaved in that way before' variety. You're at fault, that's it. And even if other people choose to joke about the incident, don't be tempted to follow their example – you're not allowed to make light of your misdemeanours.

When your hangover has subsided, use the opportunity to examine how and why you became so drunk. Whatever the reason, learn from it.

All hosts have a responsibility towards drunken guests – to protect them from other guests and from themselves. Send the drunk home in a taxi, or drive him/her there yourself. If necessary offer a bed for the night. Never abandon someone who's seriously inebriated; if anything unfortunate subsequently happens, you'll have to accept a measure of blame.

Don't become annoyed/irritated/angry with a drunk – too much alcohol can render all of us incapable of behaving properly. If you're annoyed wait until the following day and then speak your mind.

Think a member of your family, one of your friends or a work colleague has a problem with alcohol? Share your opinions with the relevant person. This isn't interference, it's concern. If the potential alcoholic does nothing to alleviate his/her condition, you should talk to other people about what might be done. Alcoholics aren't always able to look after themselves.

Drugs

First point: they're illegal. Therefore, if you take them, you're breaking the law. Second point: can you be sure what they are or where they've come from? Precisely because they're illegal, it's impossible to know the substance's contents for certain. Therefore, if you take it, you're also unlikely to know the physical consequences to yourself – both short- and long-term.

All of which implies that sensible, respectable, grown-up people never take drugs. But if you believe that, you're obviously an alien who's just landed here in a spaceship from the Planet Zog. Drugs aren't just found in the seedy basement of our social hierarchy. A lot of people – quite a few of them sensible, respectable and grown-up – take illegal substances on a regular basis and drugs turn up at even the most formal and official of occasions.

You could, of course, manage to get through life without ever seeing or trying any drugs, or ever being offered anything stronger than an aspirin. But you ought to be prepared to run into them. So the three fundamental questions that need to be answered here are: should you carry drugs with you to a party? Should you take something offered to you at such an event? Should you feel free to tuck in if everyone else, including the hosts, seems to be indulging?

Even if you've a heavy, and widely known, drug habit, it's not a good idea to bring this out and about with you like a fashion accessory. You can't be certain of other people's attitude towards your behaviour – and by the way, there are few more anti-social practices than one section of the group disappearing into another room to take drugs. So, if you must engage in this illegal activity, keep a supply of whatever's your own particular fancy at home and use it there.

What if another guest at a party/social gathering has chosen to ignore this advice and invite you to become a fellow-participant? The wisest option is probably refusal but if you're not going to be wise, at least be discreet.

Never let yourself be pressurized into taking drugs – and never pressurize someone else to do so. This must be a matter of choice. The young and emotionally vulnerable can sometimes feel under an obligation to behave in the same way as other members of their particular peer group. If you find yourself being encouraged to take drugs against your will or better judgement, the best solution is to refuse and leave immediately.

Hosts are entitled to say they don't want drugs on their premises – and to have this wish respected. You still want to smoke a joint? Go ahead and do so – in your own home.

Finally, even though taking them is unquestionably against the law, try not to become too moralistic about drugs. Lots of people become addicted to legally prescribed substances such as painkillers or sleeping pills and no one condemns them for this. Bear in mind that drugs are highly addictive – and that some of us, regrettably, do seem to have addictive personalities.

14. Clothes and Appearance

Much as you might find the idea ludicrous, throughout your life you'll be judged, at least in part, on your appearance. Particularly when meeting people for the first time, we all look at how they present themselves and draw certain conclusions from this. Superficial perhaps. But universal definitely. So you might as well make your appearance as attractive as possible, in the knowledge that doing so is more likely to help than to hinder your interaction with the rest of the world.

There are two reasons why some people don't take care of their appearance:

- They're too lazy.
- They think it's a waste of valuable time that could be devoted to more important things, such as discovering a cure for the common cold, delivering food parcels to the poor and needy of the neighbourhood, or (more often) watching tonight's episode of *Coronation Street.*

Neither of these excuses has any validity. We're all social animals (any nun who's a member of an enclosed and silent order can ignore this remark) and can therefore expect to interact with each other regularly. Good manners to our fellow men and women demand that we present ourselves as well as possible before them. To do otherwise suggests that we don't attach much value to their opinions.

Grooming

Many elements of personal grooming fall into the category of vanity. But a few can definitely be regarded as combining good manners with good sense.

THE FUNDAMENTALS

Washing regularly is certainly a prerequisite for everyone other than hermits. If you don't wash yourself thoroughly at least once a day, you're likely to smell unpleasant. This fact isn't hard to grasp and yet it's clear that some members of society still have trouble understanding the advantages of a good wash. Daily use of an anti-perspirant and/or deodorant also has strong merits, the most important of which is that it will help to keep your body odour under control. Try to appreciate that while you've no problem with the way you smell, others mightn't feel the same.

Brushing your teeth every morning and evening can be recommended; it discourages dental decay and improves your appearance. Rinsing with a mouthwash means the people you meet are far less likely to reel away looking nauseous whenever you speak. Halitosis can (and should) be treated.

Given the rising incidences of skin cancer in this country, it's advisable every morning to apply a cream with a high Sun Protection Factor (SPF) to any and every part of you left exposed to the elements. This should be done even on days when no sun is visible, and in cold climates. The cream will not only help to prevent the onset of wrinkles but possibly lengthen your life. Both are good reasons for its use.

IN ADDITION

Give a little thought (and time) to your hands. Keep them clean because they're going to be your first point of physical contact with another person. Do men still need to be reminded to wash their hands after using the lavatory? Unfortunately, yes, some of them do. That's how unpleasant germs are transmitted between people. Every day your hands touch a wide variety of different surfaces and come into contact with the equally large number of different bacteria breeding on them. You can minimize the possibility of these spreading further by washing your hands regularly. Keep your nails tidy and free of dirt. Maybe it's unfair but grubby hands suggest you'll be just as slovenly in other areas of your life.

HAIR

Don't just wash it regularly – keep it tidy and well cut. This will indicate that you want to present yourself as well as possible. Both men and women should find a good hairdresser and keep going back on a regular basis. What qualifies as regular? An appointment every month ought to keep your hair under control, with the option of quick maintenance calls during the weeks in-between. What are the characteristics of a good hairdresser? Someone who doesn't bully a client (almost all hairdressers think they know what's best for you and refuse to accept otherwise) and who gives you a haircut that's easy to manage between visits.

Look after your hairdresser (tip him/her after every visit with a bonus at Christmas) and the favour will be returned. But, on the other hand, if you're not happy with the service, don't have any qualms about taking your business elsewhere.

It's often said that hairdressers are like therapists and they certainly get to hear a lot of private information from their clients. But, also like therapists, not every hairdresser suits every client – you need to find the right one for you and this can take time.

Men who are going bald: accept your genetic predisposition is more powerful than your desire to keep a full head of hair. You can postpone the inevitable for a while, but only at the risk of making yourself look absurd in the eyes of everyone else. Surrender gracefully to your fate and keep whatever's left of your hair short and neat. Above all, never attempt to grow sections of your hair long and then use these to cover the rest of your scalp. One day soon you will be caught in a strong wind. The wind will wreak havoc. You will be left with a thin tendril of hair running down your back.

Beards, moustaches and facial hair: if you're not going to shave, keep the results clipped. It just looks better. Honestly.

A further note about men and hair: After a certain age it has an annoying habit of sprouting not just on the top of your head (unless, that is, it decides to fall out altogether) and the beard area, but also in certain other places as well, specifically your nose and your ears. Your eyebrows will suddenly start to develop long meandering offshoots too. None of this is particularly attractive to observe (it's also terribly ageing, by the way) so try to keep these developments in check. There are handy little battery-operated devices you can buy in any electrical goods shop that'll swiftly remove excess nasal and ear hair. A pair of nail scissors can be used to clip your eyebrows regularly. The result will be a better groomed, and more youthful, appearance.

MAKE-UP
It's meant to enhance your appearance, not to conceal it altogether, so don't wear too much. As a rule, where make-up's concerned, it's better to wear too little rather than too much. Watch

out for tidal lines when applying foundation (if you're worried about getting make-up on your clothes, tuck a tissue around the top of whatever you're wearing while getting ready). Try to choose lipstick that won't leave a legacy on everyone's cheek when you're social kissing. Check your make-up regularly during the day but don't apply too much more otherwise you'll end up with a thick crust on your face by evening. Make-up counters in department stores are happy to dispense advice on what will best suit you. This advice is free. Take it.

PERFUME/FRAGRANCE/AFTER-SHAVE
Not everyone will like your choice as much as you do, so keep an eye on the quality-control. A good way to wear perfume is actually not to wear it at all but to use the associated products like bath oil, shower gel or body lotion. This means your entire person carries the scent and not just a few critical (and potentially overwhelming) pulse points. Because of the increased use of chemicals in perfume, more and more people are actually allergic to fragrances. Even if they're not, it's likely that they'll find excessive application of a scent unpleasant and off-putting. Presumably not the reason you applied it in the first place?

Caring for Your Clothes

There's a valuable saying: 'keep clean is better than make clean'. This is especially true of dry cleaning which, without wishing to put anyone out of business, ought not to be encouraged too much. Dry cleaners use chemicals to remove stains from your clothes. Those chemicals, while obviously not terminally harmful, aren't terribly beneficial either over a long period of time. Even more than washing, dry cleaning tends to remove the natural life from fabric so that, while it might be cleaner, it's also rather less vibrant. Good home maintenance will minimize the need for dry cleaning. Air your clothes after wearing them and before putting them back in the wardrobe, hang them up (preferably on a wooden hanger) immediately and give them a chance to recover before wearing them again. Never wear the same item two days in a row, no matter how much you love it. Let the poor thing get some rest before putting it back on. Both you and your clothes will benefit from this policy, which also applies to ties, shoes, belts and gloves.

Rather than taking something to the dry cleaners every time a stain appears, try sorting it out yourself. There are now a wide variety of products available at your local supermarket for treating small stains at home. One of these ought to do the trick (although do remember to test the product on a hidden piece of the fabric, just to check that there won't be any adverse reaction).

The other advantage to looking after your clothes properly and treating stains yourself is that you'll save quite a lot of money, dry cleaners always seem to be horrifically expensive.

A note on tissue paper: It is one of the marvels of our age. You can never have too much tissue paper. At home, before putting clothes away in a cupboard, particularly anything prone to creasing like sweaters, fold them in tissue paper. This will absorb most of the creases and allow you simply to shake out the garment before wearing it. Similarly, when travelling, pack everything inside your suitcase in tissue paper. Creases will be minimized when you reach your destination. Remember to fold away the tissue paper and keep it in the suitcase for your return journey.

By the way, it remains true that one of the best ways to remove creases from clothes is to hang them inside a shower and then let the water run at a high temperature. The resulting steam will cause most of the creases to fall away. Just make sure not to put the clothes too close to the shower head, otherwise they risk getting soaked.

Footwear

Remember the old maxim that shop assistants and hotel concierges look at shoes to assess the worth of a customer? Of course, if that were still true today, they'd be turning away dressed-down squillionaires like Bill Gates from their doors. Nevertheless, it's worth paying some attention to whatever's on your feet. The late Diana Vreeland, a legendary editor of American *Vogue* in the 1960s, used to polish the soles of her shoes. You don't have to go that far, but do look out for scuffed heels and toes. As with clothes, the more attention you give to your shoes, the longer – and better – they will last. And, just like the rest of us, they suffer the consequences of neglect.

One way to avoid this happening to your shoes is to set aside an hour a week, perhaps while watching a favourite television programme, for polishing. That way they'll get regular attention and live longer.

Use shoe trees and put them in as soon as you've taken your shoes off (they'll keep their shape better that way). Get your shoes re-heeled as soon as the backs start to wear down. Soles should also be replaced before they become too worn. If your shoes have become wet in the rain, stuff them with newspaper to absorb as much of the moisture as possible. Change this for fresh paper after a couple of hours and repeat the process until your shoes are dry.

When you buy a new pair of shoes, particularly if they're expensive, ask for the shoe bag, which should be sold with them. Use this when you're travelling as it'll stop your shoes from becoming scuffed in the suitcase or from leaving polish marks on any clothes. Your shoes will, of course, already have shoe trees, but you can further help to keep their shape by padding them with small items of underwear, tights or socks (an additional advantage, of course, being that this then frees up a little more room in your suitcase for other things you want to bring).

Accessories

Ties: Hang it up immediately after you've taken it off (except for knitted ties, which, if hung, will stretch and should instead be rolled up). Watch out for stains – ties seem to attract them like nothing else in your wardrobe. Try lightly sponging off a dirty tie first. If this fails, either use a home stain-removal product or, as a last resort, send it to the dry cleaners.

Belts: Roll them up and lay them on a flat surface after use.

Socks: Look out for holes at the toe and heel. They'll turn up eventually. No one repairs socks any more, so socks with holes in them are seen more and more often. Minimize the effect this can have on your wardrobe by buying several pairs of the same sock at the same time. Since a hole inevitably appears in one half of a pair and not in the other, you can then team it up with another of the same kind and not have both socks go to waste. The alternative is to wear odd socks, but that piece of behaviour is confined to professional eccentrics.

Bags: When not in use, stuff them with tissue paper so that they keep their shape. Then store each of them separately inside a cloth bag (to allow the leather to 'breathe'). If you don't have any of these (as with shoes, the more expensive ones are sold with a protective bag), then an old pillowcase will serve just as well. Leather bags should occasionally be treated with an application of polish to prolong their lives.

Gloves: After taking them off, stretch out each finger and then lay the gloves flat in their pairs. Just as with all other leather goods, it's best to give them 'days off' to recover from use.

Hats: Ideally should be stored in their own hatboxes, the crowns filled with tissue paper to hold the shape in place. Then lay the boxes flat on the top of a wardrobe. You don't have any hatboxes? Again, a pillow case or something similar will be just as good. The object is to keep your hat on a flat, dust-free surface with its shape held in place.

Getting Your Appearance Right

Accept that some people have inherent flair and others don't. Some folk will be Olympic-standard swimmers and most of the rest of us are lucky not to drown in the pool. Likewise not everyone's going to win the Nobel Prize for Literature. It's just another of life's unfairnesses.

Even though you're never going to make the International Best-Dressed List, you can still make the most of what you've got. That way your appearance certainly won't cause offence and might even give pleasure.

SPORTSWEAR

For some reason this is most often worn by people who, quite clearly, have not taken any exercise in a long time. Unless you're a professional athlete, sportswear is inherently unflattering and will only make your physical disadvantages more apparent. It's a fact of life that bottoms always look bigger in a tracksuit. These should not be worn unless you're playing sports or taking exercise. A tracksuit is not permissible in company, no matter how well you know the other people. It's also worth bearing in mind two other points concerning sportswear:

Firstly, more often than not, the materials used in its manufacture are complicated mixes of man-made fibre that don't

'breathe' in the same way as natural fabrics. They are, therefore, prone to trap odours and should be washed even more
regularly than other clothing.

Secondly, despite the high prices charged, almost all sportswear
is made in Asian factories for little money and, sometimes,
under questionable conditions for the workforce. On a
point of principle, before buying any such item of clothing,
you ought to check where and how it was made.

CO-ORDINATION

This doesn't mean you're under an obligation to buy the bag
that matches the shoes. It does mean that there ought to be
some approximation in style and colour between the different
elements of what you're wearing. When getting dressed, it's best
not to try including every colour in the rainbow in your choice
of clothes. Stick to one colour or a couple of complementary
ones. Only venture beyond two colours in your appearance if
you're very confident. Be wary of patterns; in the struggle for
dominance between you and them, they're more likely to win.

BLACK

Is the preferred colour of the fashion industry and is worn by
everyone involved in the business, from magazine editors to
designers. It's easy to see why. Black has a reputation of hiding
fat but can do this, it must be pointed out, only up to a certain
point. A tent dress will still be a tent dress even when it's black.
The colour also hides dirt better than any other (not that this
should discourage you from washing your clothes regularly).
And, finally, it's anonymous; anyone meeting you is less likely to
notice that you're wearing the same black top as yesterday than
if you were wearing a red or green one that would be more
immediately memorable.

So, yes, black is incredibly convenient and transcends all seasons. But it also risks being terribly dull and unimaginative and, in daylight, can look downright dreary. It also has a nasty habit of draining all the colour from your face. Use it in moderation, and if possible, save it for nights, when black comes into its own.

One last point on this subject: there are as many shades of black as of any other colour depending on the quality of the dye and of the fabric. So you might think you're dressed entirely in the one colour but this won't necessarily be the case. Check each item in natural light to see whether it is, in fact, the same black as the others.

Still Struggling?

Consider using a personal shopper. Some of the larger department stores now offer this service for a relatively modest price (when you telephone to make an appointment, check the charge). Employing a personal shopper for a few hours can be an excellent investment, if used the right way. This means taking an active interest in what's being recommended (and take a few notes while you're about it). You pay for the personal shopper's time, whether you buy anything from the store or not, although there's usually a discount on the price of the service if you do purchase some of the suggested clothes. But you're under no obligation to buy at the end of the session.

Here are some of the questions you ought to ask your personal shopper:

- What's my correct size?
- What styles best suit my shape?
- What are my best/worst assets and how can I make the most/least of these?
- What colours can/can't I wear?
- What items of clothing should I avoid?

- In terms of the clothing recommendations now being made, should I rethink either my hair or make-up?

Treat your personal shopper as an image consultant and you'll get long-term value out of the session. If you're happy with the outcome, it's worth repeating the experience on a regular basis, particularly if you want to keep up with changing fashion trends.

Dress Codes

Are almost extinct today, but they can still come into force for formal occasions like weddings and black-tie dinners. Usually the invitation will make clear whatever sartorial demands are being made of guests. Good manners demand you meet these, whether you want to or not. And if you don't own a dinner jacket or ballgown, there are plenty of outlets happy to rent you something suitable for the occasion.

Turning up in your own freestyle interpretation of evening dress is generally not a good idea. You'll certainly look – and possibly feel – out of sync with the rest of the company. Your hosts could conclude you're being dismissive of their attitudes. No matter how much you dislike following the crowd, this isn't the best moment to express your free-spirited individuality.

Plenty of invitations today come with absolutely no guidelines about what's to be worn. The result is an event where those present look as though they've shared the contents of a second-hand clothes shop. If you suspect the party's going to be a pretty formal one but the invitation gives no indication of dress code, telephone your hosts in advance and ask for advice on the matter. They'll be delighted that you're so sensitive to their requirements and you'll be happy that what you wear is appropriate for the event.

Tip for hosts: If you do have a specific dress code in mind for your event, don't expect guests to be clairvoyant. State your wishes plainly on the invitation or phone. That way mistakes can be avoided.

Otherwise the event itself ought to give you at least some idea of suitable clothing. Your three-piece suit for a beach picnic? Jeans and a sweater for the opera? Neither sounds like the kind of style likely to endear you to the rest of the party. But if you're still left unsure of the right approach, it's probably wiser to overdress slightly rather than underdress. If you walk into a room where everyone else is in shorts and T-shirts and you're wearing a jacket and tie, it's easy to discard both and unbutton your shirt. On the other hand, you set yourself a real challenge by turning up in an old tracksuit and running shoes when the rest of the room has opted for eveningwear. And regardless of the occasion, make sure your clothing is clean; save that grubby sweater for home. Still in doubt about what to wear? Then choose something that allows you to appear smart, feel comfortable and be confident in the knowledge that it can always look more casual if necessary.

Finally, try to show an element of consideration in the way you dress. Turning up to a funeral with an exposed midriff, for example, indicates a lack of sensitivity. Different circumstances should dictate your appearance. Dress appropriately. You're the one wearing the clothes, but other people have to look at them.

Should You Comment on Other People's Appearance?

Only if you're going to say something kind. Otherwise keep your opinions to yourself. Being pass-remarkable, either to someone's face or behind his/her back is rude.

Should you give advice on someone's appearance? Only reluctantly (and only when what you say can be heavily laced with compliments). We're all naturally sensitive about how we look and can be easily wounded on the subject, even when we've asked for advice. So it's probably wisest to leave that job to the professionals.

Postscript

'Manners makyth man' according to the fourteenth-century Bishop of Winchester, William of Wyke-ham. Presumably it was only for the sake of alliteration that he didn't refer to women. In any case, his point's plain: the state of our manners is one of the features that help to define us. We're likely to make an impression on the surrounding world by showing courtesy and consideration – as well as by failing to do so.

Just as importantly, the ways in which we display courtesy and concern for other peoples' welfare is much broader than might initially appear to be the case. It's relatively easy to show good manners in formal situations where our roles are liable to be clearly delineated. But all of us can be guilty of unintentional bad manners, usually through lack of forethought and when we're in a relatively anonymous public environment. Throwing chewing gum onto the pavement or dropping cigarette butts on the street are both instances of casual bad manners because they fail to take anyone else's interests into account (remember that the next time you find a piece of gum sticking to the sole of your shoe).

Litter, which seems to be endemic in this country, is another example of unalloyed bad manners. None of us would take our rubbish and scatter it around the homes of friends; why should the same behaviour be deemed less offensive when it happens outdoors? In each case, the same want of consideration is being shown.

It's worth reiterating what is the principal characteristic of good manners: selfless courtesy. To some of us, the fortunate few, actions reflecting this trait come naturally. More often, however, courtesy is an acquired skill, one we need to learn either from our parents and teachers or through personal experience. The last of these is perhaps the best mentor; nothing beats wisdom gained first-hand. But another excellent way to improve your manners is by example. If you admire someone who always remembers to write a thank-you note after coming to dinner, why not do the same thing yourself? Imitation isn't just the sincerest form of flattery, it's also sensible where good manners are concerned. Likewise, when affronted by another person's actions or speech, make a decision not to be guilty of the same offence.

Although the circumstances of our lives have changed a great deal over the past few decades and look set to do so for some time to come, the basic tenets of good behaviour deserve to remain unaffected. Manners must stand immune to shifts in social or economic fortune. The introduction of new technology can't be allowed as an excuse for bad behaviour. I'm reminded of a scene in the 1987 film *Wall Street* where Michael Douglas is shown holding to his ear what looks like a brick: in fact, it was an early mobile phone. And he was bellowing into it, thereby proving that right from the start mobile phone users were ill mannered. In other words, no matter what happens in our lives, the same principles of courtesy and consideration apply. Manners will continue to makyth man.